AQUAPONICS
GARDENING

A Beginner's Guide to Building Your Own
Aquaponic Garden

By Tom Gordon

AQUAPONICS GARDENING

© Copyright 2019 - All rights reserved.

The content contained within this book may not be reproduced, duplicated or transmitted without direct written permission from the author or the publisher.

Under no circumstances will any blame or legal responsibility be held against the publisher, or author, for any damages, reparation, or monetary loss due to the information contained within this book. Either directly or indirectly.

Legal Notice:
This book is copyright protected. This book is only for personal use. You cannot amend, distribute, sell, use, quote or paraphrase any part, or the content within this book, without the consent of the author or publisher.

Disclaimer Notice:
Please note the information contained within this document is for educational and entertainment purposes only. All effort has been executed to present accurate, up to date, and reliable, complete information. No warranties of any kind are declared or implied. Readers acknowledge that the author is not engaging in the rendering of legal, financial, medical or professional advice. The content within this book has been derived from various sources. Please consult a licensed professional before attempting any techniques outlined in this book.

AQUAPONICS GARDENING

By reading this document, the reader agrees that under no circumstances is the author responsible for any losses, direct or indirect, which are incurred as a result of the use of information contained within this document, including, but not limited to, — errors, omissions, or inaccuracies.

# AQUAPONICS GARDENING

TABLE OF CONTENTS

Introduction vi

Part I - Getting Down to Basics x

   Chapter One - What is Aquaponic Gardening and How Does it Work? 1

   Chapter Two - The Great Matchup: 5

   Aquaponics vs Hydroponics Gardening 5

   Chapter Three - What are The Benefits of Aquaponic Gardening? 11

Part II - Roll Up Your Sleeves, Let's Get Down to Basics 17

   Chapter Four - Types of Aquaponic Systems 18

   Chapter Five - Setting Up Your Aquaponic Garden 29

   Chapter Six - Setting Up Your Tech-Savvy Aquaponic Garden 41

   Chapter Seven - Setting Up a Towering Aquaponic Garden 51

   Chapter Eight - Setting Up the Easiest Aquaponic Garden 60

   Chapter Nine - What's In Your Water? 66

   (More than You Ever Wanted to Know About pH) 66

Part III - Filling Your Aquaponic System with Life 76

   Chapter Ten - What's On the Menu? 77

   86

Chapter Eleven - For a Small System, Grow a Lettuce Bowl 87

Chapter Twelve - For a Large System, Grow a Vegetable Plate 94

Chapter Thirteen - How Do I Start Growing Plants? . 104

Chapter Fourteen - Maintenance and Pest Prevention 110

Chapter Fifteen - Commercial Applications of Aquaponic Gardening 117

Chapter Sixteen - Make Great Food 128

Part IV - The Science Behind Aquaponic Gardening 144

Chapter Seventeen - Glossary of Terms 145

Final Words 170

INTRODUCTION

If you like to grow your food, you probably love the feel of soil and revel in the joy of harvesting your crops. Gardens give us pleasure. Gardens date back to our earliest ancestors finding edibles in the wild and learning how to transplant them into a plot of ground. The hanging gardens of Babylon testify to the sense of wonder a garden brings.

What's more, gardening offers other benefits, such as stress reduction, exercise, and stockpiling all that valuable Vitamin D obtained from sunshine. (Vitamin D deficiencies are linked to an increase of heart attacks, type 1 diabetes, and osteoporosis.) Another obvious benefit is the savings factor. In the summer, we eat out of the garden and reduce our grocery bills. I preserve extra for winter use as well. In fact, I cannot imagine life without a garden. However, gardening is not always easy.

Harsh climatic conditions, such as winter weather with a short summer, or life in a desert area, often makes growing your own food a challenge. Plus, watering a garden gets expensive. Maintaining the soil quality can get complicated, buying fertilizer and worrying about keeping it ready for the next season of growth. The good news is, none of that is necessary.

The world of aquaponic gardening beckons you to a new way of cultivating and harvesting your own food, and it's not as hard as it sounds. I know. When I first started researching aquaponic gardening, I was overwhelmed in less than an hour. I have to what? Doesn't it smell? Fish! Ugh! *I don't think so!*

Slowly that distaste grew to grudging respect. The more I learned, the more I wanted to know. After combing countless books and articles, I finally felt ready to embark on this new adventure, but my table lay piled with articles and heaps of paper mocking every attempt at instilling order. When I needed to refresh my memory, I had to rifle through the mess and it was unwieldy at best, a disaster more often than I cared to admit.

Putting all of that information into a format at my fingertips became the genesis of this book. By the time I put it all together, my own floating gardens were a testament to the return of the wonders of Babylon—in my eyes, at least. My neighbors loved the vegetables I was able to share with them, so their praise was hearty as well.

You too can grow your own water-based garden, and it's not as hard as you think. A big plus was my first hand experience in proving it was not stinky after all! I wouldn't have guessed it, but it's true. A properly managed aquaponic garden produces less smell than an aquarium, because the ammonium levels are consistently maintained at the proper level, as opposed to a fish tank no one wants to clean on Monday, Tuesday, or any other day of the week.

To make it easier for friends and family (and that includes you, gentle reader, for you are a new friend), I'm sharing what I've learned. I want to provide you with a more readable, yet complete guide, for following in my footsteps. I'm expecting that some of you have never gardened before, so I'm offering you basic instructions, plus an indexed glossary for added detail. Perhaps you live in an urban area and have never had the opportunity to garden; you'll find aquaponic gardening is perfect for rooftops. Perhaps you live in a climate that doesn't support the required growing season for tomatoes; indoor aquaponic gardening is perfect for you. Don't be afraid to hop on the bandwagon and take advantage of this new option that is igniting the gardening community. I want to give you all the information you need:

- You need to know what aquaponic gardening is and is not.
- You need some convincing before you jump into the water, and so does your family!
- You need to learn about the systems available, and how to choose the best system for your home and garden.
- You need to learn how to set it up, how to maintain it, and how it works.
- Most of all, you need a textbook with a dictionary to learn a lot of new terms and the scientific background to share with disbelieving family and friends. To that end, I have highlighted in bold the terms defined and expounded upon in the glossary at the end of the book. I promise I won't overload you with too much information too quickly, exploding your head and causing you to

cast the book aside in despair. Don't worry, we're in this together.

This is your go-to book for creating your own aquaponic garden, a garden you can use year-round, indoors or out, always growing your lettuce bowl or vegetable plate. That's right. With your aquaponic garden, your dinner makins are just steps away. Are you ready to dig in? Let's do this together!

PART I

GETTING DOWN TO BASICS

CHAPTER ONE

WHAT IS AQUAPONIC GARDENING AND HOW DOES IT WORK?

If you're a gardener, you've experienced the joy of planting and harvesting food for the table. Me? I love the beginning and the end...but not so much the middle. You know what I mean: endless weed pulling, regular watering and fertilizing, pest control and manicuring the garden. What if I told you there was a way to bypass that middle step? That would be great, right?

Aquaponic gardening is water-based, not soil-based. It incorporates a built-in source of fertilizing. It's a perfect world where weeding *never happens*. Your garden is a delight for the eyes, and you do it all with little daily effort.

But here's the trick: are you familiar with **symbiosis**? You're going to create a symbiotic relationship between plant and animal. First, you'll set up a water tank with some kind of fish (and we'll get to that), but there are soooo many types of fish, depending on what you want to grow and the size available. Then, you'll create a nutrient-laden water supply (**nutrient film**) and a means for distributing it. Then, you'll plant your seedlings in containers that receive constant water...

The end result? The fish provide the fertilizer. The plants keep the water clean, and you enjoy the harvest. The way you create that optimal brew and the way you distribute it can be derived from several different forms of aquaponic gardening, but the concept holds true for everyone.

A key factor is its **sustainability**. An aquaponic garden is meant to function on its own with a minimal amount of effort. It takes a little information and some work to set it up, a little time to create that lovely nutrient-laden water, but it's all part of the joy in building your very own masterpiece of fish and produce, meshed together in a mutually beneficial ecosystem.

Yes, it's that simple. I expected it to be a daunting procedure. I mean, at first glance, I thought it sounded fishy (bad pun), but the more I researched and put into practice the tips I was learning, the easier it got. The information overload at the beginning left my head spinning, but as I began to take notes, I realized that some people just love to make things difficult. Aquaponic gardening was meant to be *simple*.

AQUAPONICS GARDENING

★ As we progress I hope you're looking up our keywords in the glossary. That's where you'll find all the extra information on each term. Think of this book as a sort of *Aquaponics for Dummies*, with an encyclopedia available as you're ready for more information. I'm including links to help you every step of the way!

You exercise all power in the process. You decide on the system that fits your budget and where you'll put it. You decide on the kind of fish to stock in your water. I began with goldfish, an endless source of delight for children, with a ready supply of salad greens, grown just off the kitchen. You decide whether to grow vertically or horizontally. You decide what to grow.

Best of all, you decide whether this is a hobby, a way to supplement your cupboards, or a way to supplement your income. A healthy market for microgreens is a gateway from experimenting, to then expanding, and then marketing your produce to local restaurants. Winter vegetables straight from the garden to the table are within your reach. Begin small, grow as you are ready.

AQUAPONICS GARDENING

Chapter Summary

- Aquaponics is growing fish to nourish vegetables, and growing vegetables to clean the water for the fish. This is a mutually beneficial arrangement.
- Aquaponics is **sustainable**, a *green* way to live in harmony with mother nature.
- Aquaponics is adaptable for every living situation, from growing a lettuce bowl in your apartment to a commercial enterprise replacing your day job.

In the next chapter, you will learn the differences between hydroponics and aquaponics. By being well versed, you can embark on your project with full confidence in your plan.

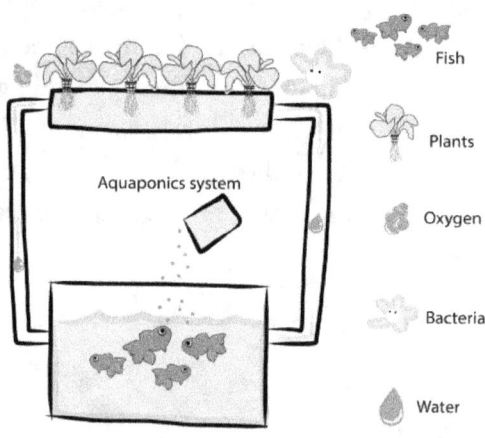

CHAPTER TWO

THE GREAT MATCHUP: AQUAPONICS VS HYDROPONICS GARDENING

They sound a lot alike, don't they? **Hydroponics** and Aquaponics? They are similar in one way, but vastly different where it counts. Hydroponics means, literally, grown in water. If you take the words aquaculture + hydroponics and put them together, you get aquaponics. Let's look at the two processes in more detail to see why one will be better for you over another.

Ditch the soil. Both systems offer growing a garden without soil. This represents a huge benefit. Soil becomes stagnant after years of cultivation, requiring a lot of fertilizer and/or rotation of crops. Simply replacing the soil during repetitive seasons of indoor growth becomes expensive On top of that, soil is easily contaminated with spores or pests laying eggs, perpetuating all of the diseases from one season to the next. Growing in soil almost requires an outdoor garden, and living in a climate zone with harsh winters means you can only grow your veggies half of the year. Both systems offer value in growing without soil.

Instead of soil, you'll grow your plants in a biosystem of specially cultured beneficial bacteria, and your very own circle of life will sustain both fish and plants. This healthy substitute for dirt is simple to produce, and you'll wonder why you never tried aquaponic gardening before.

Fertilize the water. Both systems require nutrient-based water for plant growth. Hydroponic gardening employs chemical nutrients, which represents constant overhead. You may obtain your growing medium from any number of suppliers, but let's face it: the uncertain role of chemicals in cancer and birth defects is generating headlines around the world. In aquaponics, you may grow *organic* vegetables through natural fertilizer produced by fish swimming around the tank. *The advantage goes to aquaponics.*

Design the right space. Both systems require light and a floor strong enough to withstand some pretty hefty weight. I was clueless. I imagined a sweet little aquarium with plants above it, and was shocked to realize a twenty gallon aquarium weighs a whopping 225 pounds. A concrete floor in the basement sounded smart, but I was hooked on the idea of cute goldfish and had a 14-ft bay window in the dining room, so the scales became my enemy.

★ Figure about one inch of fish per gallon of water. If I have a fifty gallon tank, you'll need fifty one-inch goldfish. As they grow, that number decreases.

My research suggested that I needed at least a fifty gallon tank, so I had to adjust my weight limits to six hundred pounds. If space and weight are an issue for you, *hydroponics has the advantage in this case.*

Both systems are going to affect your utility bills. The difference between them is that in hydroponics, the water may not be recycled. In aquaponics, the water must be recycled to formulate the rich growth medium to fertilize the plants. A high water bill would make it cheaper to buy the produce at the market, which makes *aquaponics preferable.*

Both require a growth medium that serves as an anchor for the plants, helps regulate temperature, and provides constant nourishment. In aquaponics, **hydroton** is a popular form made from clay, but see Chapter Four to read more on that subject. I wanted to get a product I was accustomed to using, but all of them were on the no-no list: sand, vermiculite, peat moss, wood chips, and pearlite. On the plus side, this represented a one-time purchase, and I could live with that. I see no strong value of one system over the other, because both require a mix to hold the plant.

Both systems require an investment in setting up the apparatus. A hydroponic garden is cheaper to start if you employ a **wicking** or water culture system. Both require a more complex design for some setups, and hydroponics equals the cost of aquaponics when you add a sump pump and additional piping. Aquaponics requires an investment in fish, but the cost will be less than continually buying chemical fertilizers for the water. In this case, *the plus goes to aquaponics.*

However, the learning curve is definitely higher for aquaponic gardening. Because you are dealing with live organisms to create the fertilizer for your plants, it takes time and experimentation to get the right mix for ideal growth. If you require instant gratification, go with hydroponics. If you like a challenge, like to putter with details, and are willing to wait for results, go with aquaponics. For ease and learning *the plus goes to hydroponics.*

AQUAPONICS GARDENING

Chapter Summary

If you've been keeping score, you already know why aquaponics is favored over hydroponics with homesteaders and survivalists, as well as a growing number of hobby gardeners.

- Aquaponics is cheaper than hydroponics since it recycles water usage.
- Aquaponics is cheaper than hydroponics since a one time investment of fish fertilizes the plants for years, versus buying a constant supply of chemical fertilizers.
- Hydroponics is easier to learn and operate than aquaponics.

In the next chapter, you will learn why aquaponics is the best thing since sliced bread. Just why are homesteaders and survivalists the world over head over heels in love with aquaponic gardening?

AQUAPONICS GARDENING

CHAPTER THREE

WHAT ARE THE BENEFITS OF AQUAPONIC GARDENING?

We already discussed the obvious benefits of aquaponic over hydroponic growing systems. Perhaps you still aren't convinced it's worth the time and hassle to try it out. Read on!

My number one plus for aquaponic gardening is that it is 100% organic. If you harbor any hopes of profiting from your experiment, grow organically certified vegetables. In the United States, the growth of the organic marketplace has mushroomed to more than $39 billion in reported profits. I found that obtaining a certified organic status was an easy process, and I was able to get the paperwork online.

★ Even if you choose not to be registered organic, you can tell buyers your produce is *organically grown*. It's a subtle differentiation, but one that satisfies most consumers.

AQUAPONICS GARDENING

Suppose you don't want to sell any of your produce? Still, it's **organic.** Knowing you and your loved ones are eating food with no hormones, chemicals, pesticides, or **genetically modified organisms** (GMOs), is measured in peace of mind. To many, organic foods offer better flavor and texture. And let's face it, nothing is more organic than home grown fertilizer provided via watering from a fish tank. I obviously am a proponent of organic gardening. Beyond that, I'm all for safe food. Recalls, salmonella scares, and bioterrorism cease to worry me when I produce my own food.

A second benefit of aquaponic gardening is needing less water to grow your food. In a closed system of repurposed water, this is a huge benefit. In normal outdoor summer gardening, I stand and hold a hose about an hour a day. Some of that water gets sucked into the atmosphere, some of it runs off, and all of it costs money. Not only will you save money by not manually watering your plants, but your sustainable aquaponic garden recycles the water in your system. Researchers estimate that aquaponic gardens require 90% less water than their traditional backyard counterparts.

A third benefit is the ability to extend the growing season. I live in a temperate zone with hot summers and icy cold winters. I can extend my lettuce bowl crops with a **high tunnel**, but obviously that's expensive and a lot of work. The plastic needs to be replaced every couple of years. A cheap plastic doesn't filter the ultraviolet rays, so there's a few more dollars when going for quality. I still have to utilize row covers in the very early spring and very late fall. Some winters I lose my crop all together. Hail storms and heavy winds wreak havoc on my system. Moving the winter growing indoors into a sustainable system was huge for me.

A fourth benefit was the versatility of aquaponic gardening. It eliminated all concerns over where and when I chose to garden. I could put together a system in my backyard, basement, or living room dependent on individual circumstances. Even if you live in an area with long winters or desert conditions, you can still have a garden.

A fifth benefit was how easy it was to maintain my vegetable garden. It was waist high, so I experienced no back-breaking weed pulling. As a matter of fact, I no longer had to pull weeds at all.

A sixth benefit was being able to streamline my efforts. Like you, my life was and remains a perfect storm of activity at times. Being able to institute a system four to six times more productive per square foot was a huge consideration. I could densely plant my seedlings much closer together, being able to plant twice as many seedlings in the same space as before. Add to that the fact that harvest times came sooner, since the plants grew faster with consistent watering and fertilizing. I liked working smarter, not harder.

A seventh benefit was the opportunity to grow my enterprise. Aquaponic gardening is scalable, meaning you can start with a ten gallon aquarium of goldfish and you can expand your size at will. Utilize the same mechanics and enlarge or reduce your enterprise based on your own schedule and gardening needs.

And last but certainly not least, an eighth benefit of aquaponic gardening rested in the potential of being able to eat my source of fertilizer. True, I was immediately enamored by the idea of growing goldfish, but I soon saw the wisdom in upgrading to a system growing tilapia. Yum! Aquaculture took on a whole new meaning when I was able to grow two crops with one expenditure of effort.

In retrospect, I found so many reasons to embark on this quest to learn and implement aquaponics. If you agree, it's time to get down to specifics.

AQUAPONICS GARDENING

Chapter Summary

Looking for the benefits of aquaponic gardening?

- Organic gardening at its finest
- Lower water consumption
- Longer growing seasons
- Lower water bills
- Widespread application
- Less work
- Increased productivity
- Scalable enterprise
- More fish dinners

In the next chapter you will learn the basic types of aquaponic gardening systems.

AQUAPONICS GARDENING

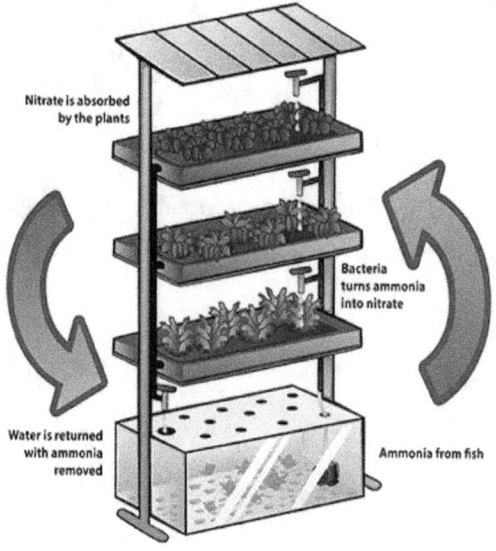

PART II

ROLL UP YOUR SLEEVES, LET'S GET DOWN TO BASICS

CHAPTER FOUR

TYPES OF AQUAPONIC SYSTEMS

While this is the most intensive system of growing and providing food on the planet, it does require some special knowledge. You will be meshing a hydroponic (water-based) system with an aquaculture (animal-based) system, and must choose the design that will best meet your needs. You need to know the living requirements of three different kinds of organisms: plants, fish, and bacteria. Finally, you need to build and wire a system that regulates the water for optimal growth factors. That may sound like a lot, but don't be frightened. We'll go through these issues one by one.

The popularity of aquaponic gardening is on the rise, and as you go through this chapter, look for online communities and support groups who can offer you additional firsthand experience for your location. You are entering a worldwide phenomenon and there is no need to reinvent the wheel. You may be able to visit several gardens; comparing and contrasting the features you like.

AQUAPONICS GARDENING

If you are wanting to take a stab at aquaponic gardening, your first decision must be choosing the type of system you want to use. The simplest experiment would be using a sun pond where plants float on the surface with submerged roots. Of course, most of us don't have ponds and are immediately looking at a more sophisticated setup.

Every aquaponic system must include five basic elements:

- a fish tank
- a plant bed
- a means of handling solid waste
- a **biofilter**
- pumps for circulating and aerating water

And these are only the most basic requirements. If you're like me, you'll want a few more bells and whistles, because what's the point of putting in all the effort, only to be met with failure because you decided to go bare bones? For starters, let's look at the types of gardens and then return to these five topics with a little more basic information under our belts.

First, look at space limitations, cost, and ease of maintenance. To help you narrow down your choices, I am describing the options by three classifications: growing a lettuce bowl, growing a vegetable plate, and commercial enterprises. While many a summer found me selling produce at a local farmer's market, I wasn't convinced I wanted to implement an aquaponic garden on that large of a scale, but I nevertheless wanted to look at all options, as will you.

If you are growing a *lettuce bowl*, a **nutrient film technique** (NFT) is your best option. Don't get bogged down in how to build one just yet, but you need enough details to make an informed decision. This is perfect for small plants with shallow roots. Microgreens, all types of lettuce, strawberries, and herbs fall into this category.

The NFT is great for a DIY kind of enterprise. Basically, you will set up your fish tank with a small sump pump running fish water through a PVC pipe with holes drilled into it, and then insert seedlings into a small net attached to each hole. The net offers your plants structure and keeps them from falling through to the bottom of the fish tank. Your plants will extend their roots toward the nutrient laden water, absorbing nutrients much like a paper towel absorbs moisture on a kitchen countertop. A key element is creating a system with a trickle of consistent water flow, rather than a stagnant pool of dank smelly water. These tubes take the place of those traditional grow trays dominating garden centers every spring.

Your NFT system can be as large or small as you want it, as sophisticated or simple as your budget demands. Large sheets of Styrofoam will work just as well as holes drilled into PVC pipes. We'll cover the actual construction in the next chapter, but you want to factor the basic principles into your choice of set up.

Another simple form of watering a nutrient film is an **ebb and flow** system of flooding the growing bed, then letting it drain back down into the fish tank. Your roots are saturated with the nutrient rich water and exposed to it for a longer period of time, in contrast to the dripping method of percolating your water and feeding small amounts to your produce constantly. It requires proximity several times a day or a timer to regulate consistent watering.

A key feature of a garden fed with a nutrient film is creating a bed of growth medium in which the water is made perfect for both fish and plants. It should run through the growth media on its way up to the plants, and then trickle back down to the fish after the plants have done their magic.

A **deep water culture** (DWC) has been valuable throughout history. Early Aztecs (around 1000 BC) created rafts and grew plants resting on their surfaces, with roots dangling in the water. They circulated their water and waste around the rafts to fertilize their crops. Some Asian cultures used ponds and natural sources of water for growing their food, and also created floating gardens. It worked especially well for growing rice.

However, you don't need to live by a pond or lake. You can accomplish the same technique with tanks to hold your water. This is perhaps the simplest and least expensive form of aquaponic gardening. Your plants may rest on the surface of the tank, roots fully submerged into the water. You still have the option of inserting canals and pumping the water through two tanks, but you can certainly start small and increase your level of complexity with experience.

You will obviously still need a fish tank to act as a home for your guests of honor. You may still need a **biofilter** to transform fish waste into nutrients for your plants. You will probably want a filter to remove solid waste or plant material from infiltrating or clogging your system. If you install canals, you will need a pump to force water through your system to ensure the water is being recirculated. As with all fish tanks, you'll need an aerator to maintain a high level of oxygen for your environment.

This is scalable, meaning you can use either an aquarium, a stock tank, or plastic tubs. You only need to maintain the correct proportions of volume, fish, and plants to achieve the desired results. I've split up the requirements in maintaining your enterprise from the mechanics of setting it up so your eyes don't glaze over with an information overload. I promise you: it's not hard and you can do this. For now, just decide on how you want to grow your plants.

AQUAPONICS GARDENING

A **media based system** is the option of choice if you want to grow larger plants like tomatoes, zucchini, and other items for your *vegetable plate*. It will function more like your traditional backyard garden, since plants will grow in small pebbles replacing soil. In an aquaponic media-based garden you will incorporate a five step process:

1. Choose a fish tank. You can repurpose an old bathtub in the basement with grow lights or have an aquarium next to a window, but first and foremost, you need a place for fish. The fish eat food and produce waste.
2. Most aquariums already need small pumps for aerating the water. You will also install a small sump pump to cycle water waste to your plants.
3. Your gardening container, ideally about twelve inches deep, will house the growing medium. You will need to purchase some form of **LECA** (Large Expanded Clay Aggregate), a product akin to **hydroton** pebbles, which will provide a petri dish for culturing bacteria from your fish waste. This is where the magic happens. The bacteria convert fish waste laden with ammonia into fertilizer, a nitrate your plants will use for growth. You are creating a sustainable biofilter and your own mini **nitrogen cycle**.

4. Your plants will absorb the nitrates and, in the process, purify the water.
5. Clean water is siphoned back to the fish.

Your final consideration in designing your setup is deciding on how and where you are going to grow your plants. Is this going to be in the backyard? Of course, your climate and your goals dictate the answer to this question, but it bears an impact on the type of system you're creating. Will it be in a **high tunnel**? Will it be indoors with natural light? Will it rest in the basement with **grow lights**? Will you be growing plants vertically? A towering garden works especially well in apartments with limited space and for the artist who wants to create not just a garden, but a work of art.

These questions all figure into your choice of design, and need to be weighed. I recommend looking at the pictures throughout the book , reading through each of the chapters describing how the systems are built, and then sitting down with a pad and paper. Crystallize your needs and hopes, sketch out a plan.

Even though we own a high tunnel, I opted for indoor construction. In our frigid winters, the high tunnel extends the growing season, but when the first freeze hits, all plants go dormant. Only mature plants can be harvested, and then, only in the afternoon as the plants perk up and shrug off the frost. Installing an aquaponic garden in my high tunnel wouldn't provide the kind of fresh vegetables I wanted.

Since I have a dining room with lots of southern exposure and floor to ceiling windows, I opted for an indoor system without grow lights. I also wanted to keep it simple, so I decided on using hydroton pellets in small plastic pots.

If you harbor any qualms about your lighting situation, you can always find a light intensity meter and test the area you want to use for your garden. After putting a lot of time, effort and some expense into setting up your aquaponic garden, you certainly don't want to find out you chose a dark corner where nothing will grow.

Do you see how to work through the decision making process? Take a moment right now to answer questions as your friend or partner might ask them, and come up with your own idea of where you're headed. It's that step of imagining the garden that precedes the construction and planting of any garden.

Chapter Summary

Deciding on the type of aquaponic garden you want to install isn't hard once you look at all of the options.

- A nutrient fed system is perhaps the easiest unit to design and operate with success. It includes options of consistent watering through a drip system or periodic flooding with an ebb and flow system.
- A deep water culture requires more planning and preparation, but can be very economical. Its operation requires developing a feel for the perfect watery stew, creating it by running the water through a media bed, and then letting your vegetable roots dally in the water constantly.
- A media bed requires the largest cost outlay and takes the most space. It closely resembles the gardens you may have grown in your backyard, the soil being replaced with the growth medium. Each vegetable is planted in a bed of pebbles.

In the next few chapters you will learn how to construct your aquaponic garden. I'll give you all of the details required in four types of gardens, and I recommend you read each of the chapters before settling on one idea over another. Once you have a basic idea of

AQUAPONICS GARDENING

what is involved in each type of garden it will be easier to choose one. Let's enter the garden gate!

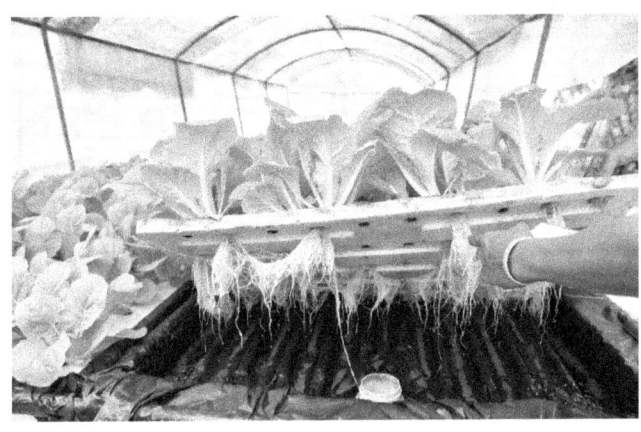

AQUAPONICS GARDENING

CHAPTER FIVE

SETTING UP YOUR AQUAPONIC GARDEN

If You Love a Great Find

Aquaponics is a DIY paradise, so if you're of that mentality, you're going to love this chapter. If you aren't, don't get horrified. I'll cover all of the many ways you can do this and, rest assured, one will appeal to you and work in your circumstances.

The most basic and easiest way to get started is to buy a kit, but some of you are going to want to cobble together a system from repurposed components, and others are going to design a 5th Avenue kind of apparatus. Any kind of receptacle will work as long as it meets these requirements: It must be strong enough to hold water *and* support the growth medium at the outset. It needs to be made from food grade material, safe for fish and plants and bacteria. You will need to be able to connect it to other parts with easily obtained plumbing supplies from a local hardware store. Also, you may need to use a pond liner if it's not watertight by nature.

Now, your system doesn't have to be expensive from the outset, but it will take time: time to build it, time to stock it, and time to develop the right environment to support growth. What is your time worth? Personally, If you live with a Mr. Handyman who would love to sink his teeth into this project, you'll make a good team.

Begin by choosing your site with care. Then begin to start your system. Decide how many fish you want to have and how many plants you want to grow. Count the cost. Don't forget to add in the tank, beds, media, plumbing, lights, pump and aerator, fish, seeds or seedlings, testing equipment, fish food, power, and water. These are basic elements. Sure, if I irrigate the beds and erect canals, I might be able to get by without a sump pump, but just how diligent am I? See what I mean?

Scenario Number One: The DIY Scrounger

So you're a do-it-yourselfer. I can spot you a mile away, and admire your ingenuity. But let's face it: you're not just any do-it-yourselfer. You like to scrounge for your materials and go your own way. You can save a significant amount of moolah by utilizing what you have or finding what you need at thrift stores and junkyards. You'll invest more of yourself and less of your cash, and

AQUAPONICS GARDENING

your new little world will be your baby. There's nothing wrong with that.

Let's begin with some of your basic considerations and how you might choose to build your system. Seamless tanks will last longer than ones with seams. Acrylic tanks will have less of a tendency to leak and should you, heaven forbid, have to move your setup, they are also less breakable. You may fancy repurposing an old bathtub, or want to achieve a beautiful system showcasing the latest technology.

Look at all of the basic components in the systems you investigate. Some require changing cartridges, and that will be an added item to monitor and keep in supply. Since you're handy, only get a pump you can fix if it breaks down or the motor goes out. You can significantly reduce costs if you can extend its lifespan. If you plan on harvesting fish as well as crops, you'll need tanks for breeding purposes. Draw out your plan and make sure you have every component covered.

You think you're ready to start building, but hold your horses. Think and rethink every detail. What shape is your tank? Many suggest that a round tank provides better water circulation and complain that a square or rectangular tank leave more solid waste that must be cleaned out regularly. If you're the artsy type, remember that all those curves and angles represent dead spaces that will decrease your system's efficiency.

AQUAPONICS GARDENING

As you refine your plans and sketch out your design, you'll need to start your shopping list. This represents your most basic needs for a simple system.

1. Find or purchase your fish tank. This is your bottom tank. Make sure it's large enough for both your water needs, but also sturdy enough to support the plant tank, depending upon your design. Personally, I'm salivating over a new outdoor system for the summer with a clawfoot bathtub, but that may be a larger chunk of change than I'm willing to invest. If you're stashing this in the basement with grow lights, it doesn't have to be decorative. If you're creating a visual masterpiece, you can still scrounge for your tank, but it will cost you a tiny bit more.
2. Order a pH test kit.
3. Find or purchase the growing tank. This needs to rest above your fish tank. You can either use two containers that rest upon one another, or fashion a stand to hold the upper tank. Bear in mind that it can rest directly above your fish tank, or stand next to the fish tank, but gravity being a law of the universe, it needs a resting place *above* the first tank.
4. Order your growing medium. As a newbie, I recommend you spring for either **hydroton** or some other version of **LECA** pebbles for your media bed. In creating you own little universe—a living ecosystem—so many things can go

AQUAPONICS GARDENING

wrong, killing your fish and then your plants. I heartily recommend staying with the tried and true on your first go round.

5. You need to purchase an **aeration pump** for the fish tank. Remember that your fish need oxygen.
6. You need to purchase a small **sump pump** to move your water. I've gone into a lot of detail on this in the glossary, because this is the key to your new ecosystem. If you fail to circulate the water, your grow medium doesn't flourish with bacteria, your ammonia never breaks down, and your plants end up living in an arid wasteland without fertilizer. You need a reliable sump pump.
7. Tubing for circulating the water as it is pumped.
8. Gravel. Expect to purchase 2.5 pounds for each five gallons of water.
9. A drill with three different sizes of bits: ½", ¼", and 3/16".
10. Electrical tape
11. Scissors
12. Screws, nuts and bolts, and washers for connecting some kinds of parts.
13. Fish
14. Styrofoam for a growing platform your plants rest upon. (Rafting is the easiest and simplest system. I'll cover channels in the next section for the DIY Engineer.

15. Grow lights to take the place of Mother Nature's sunlight. You may be thinking you can skimp on this. Don't. **Grow lights** represent one of the three basic components of photosynthesis. Your plants need ample sunlight, whether it's from Mother Nature or her buddy building the aquaponic garden.
16. Plants

When you have your shopping list researched and purchased, you're ready for assembly. I hope you're a word person, because I'm going to describe what you're making. I know a lot of you will be saying, "But I need a picture!" Here's the problem with that mentality. A picture is a great guide for comparing your final setup, and I'll give you some links to look at, but you want to *understand* your system inside and out. That requires digesting words and knowing *why* you put things together in a particular way.

Read my instructions before you get too antsy and look for a picture. Remember, you're investing time and money in this endeavor, and you need to understand how each part of the assembly is supposed to function to be able to troubleshoot for problems. There are several basic options available for all of you scroungers, and I'm going to describe just one or two before I give you links.

AQUAPONICS GARDENING

1. Set up your fish tank. If your tank doesn't stand on the floor, it needs a sturdy base. If you are using a wooden crate, put in a durable pond liner. My dining room floor is wood, so I wanted a carpet and plastic liner underneath. My experience proves that water splashes and, as Murphy's law suggests: "anything that can go wrong will go wrong," cautioning safety.
2. Wash your gravel and line the bottom of the tank.
3. Insert your sump pump with hosing rising above the water level. The amount of hose you need depends on just where your growing bed lives. If it's right above the aquarium you need less. If you're running a system adjacent to the aquarium you need more. Give yourself an ample amount of hose.
4. Fill your tank with the desired level of water.
5. Attach your aerator if it isn't submersible, or add it to the bottom if it is meant to be inside of the tank.
6. Measure your water temperature and pH level. I recommend using a spiral notebook with columns drawn for recording your daily readings. It's helpful at the outset to track your progress. Leave space on the side of each line to note changes you've made so that you can make correlations and draw correct conclusions on how your system is affected by each change.

AQUAPONICS GARDENING

7. Welcome your fish. Just starting out, expect to have one fish per plant for every 10 gallons of water. As your system becomes more efficient, you can expand and play with these numbers. As my experience proves, you can start small with one system, and then expand to another system for the outdoors, and a third with grow lights in the basement.

8. Place your growing bed above the height of the tank. The simplest structure will be a layer of styrofoam resting on top of the tank. Drill holes to release water back into the fish tank. You may prefer a secondary base with your garden bed sitting beside the aquarium. I think it looks nice and it's easier to feed and deal with the fish when the surface of the aquarium isn't obscured by your plant raft.

9. Figure out how, where, or if you need to install **grow lights**. Don't take chances on this. You may have adequate lighting, but if you don't, you're going to waste a month or more of effort in finding that out, evidenced by failing plant growth. At that point you'll be scratching your head and trying to figure out how to cobble together something that works. My best advice is to plan for it from the outset.

10. Whatever kind of receptacle you're growing your plants within, fill it with the soaked LECA pellets or Hydroton. Allow time for all the pebbles to

settle into the base without floating to the surface. You don't want to clog your pump with pebbles getting sucked into the hose, getting lodged in a delicate mechanism.

11. Decide how you're growing your plants. You can cut holes in the Styrofoam and let the roots dangle straight into the water, but you'll need little grow nets to hold the roots and offer structure. You could also cut holes in plastic pots, resting them in the watery base. Personally, I favor the pots. At the outset I was particularly leery of losing little plants into the aquarium or having pellets slip down through the holes. I come from a long line of dirt farmers, so I wanted a method mimicking the process I have always used.

12. Add your seeds or plants. For your maiden voyage I recommend getting small starts from a nursery. Wash the dirt out of the roots, and plant them.

Now, are you ready for some pictures? Here are a few setups created by survivalists and scroungers and I'll list them in the order of my preference. I think you'll see that with some imagination and by *understanding* the steps above, you can combine elements from each into something uniquely you.

Forget that this picture has no fish. It demonstrates the sytrofoam rafting technique of a small indoor aquaponic setup. I particularly like the gravitational flow of this basement application, complete with a grow light. Notice how this stacking system utilizes less floor space, helpful if you live in a small home or apartment. Look at this stylish model! Antiques offer a certain flair, but I like to grow more vegetables than this...but I love that look! I think you're getting the picture of just how simple and economic aquaponic gardening can be, but what if you want a more sophisticated system?

AQUAPONICS GARDENING

Chapter Summary

Survivalists, preppers, minimalists, and crusty old farmers love to cobble together a system on a dime. So do economically minded housewives and people who love the feeling of a simple system.

- Using repurposed supplies lets you put more money into fish and less into structure.
- If you build it from scratch, you'll know how to maintain or repair parts that later demand your attention.
- The more unexpected your design, the more friends and family will rave over it.

In the next chapter, you will learn what the nerds among us love the most—techie and detailed designs.

AQUAPONICS GARDENING

CHAPTER SIX

SETTING UP YOUR TECH-SAVVY AQUAPONIC GARDEN

If You Obsess Over Design

Some of you have engineering minds. You dream big, and I don't blame you. I favor a more tailored system myself, because I think it increases efficiency and proves how valuable aquaponic gardening really is. Since this isn't a cheap endeavor, talk it over and see what you can afford, where you can cut costs, and how you might streamline the process.

An engineering mind works with precision. You like facts and figures. You always have a blueprint in place before you begin building anything. Does this sound familiar to you? You're either an engineer or you're married to one, and this chapter is for you. An engineer likes all the nitty gritty details, and that attention to detail is what is going to make your garden a marvel.

AQUAPONICS GARDENING

1. Find or purchase your fish tank. This is your bottom tank. Make sure it's large enough for your water needs, but also sturdy enough to support the plant tank, depending upon your design. If you're stashing this in the basement with grow lights, it doesn't have to be decorative. If you're creating a visual masterpiece, pay for a tank that reflects your personality. You'll pay a little more, but you'll love it.
2. Order a pH test kit.
3. Find or purchase the growing tank. This needs to rest above your fish tank. You can either use two containers which rest upon one another, or fashion a stand to hold the upper tank. All engineers know gravity is a law of the universe, so the grow bed needs a resting place above the first tank.
4. Order your growing medium. As a newbie, I recommend you spring for either **hydroton** or some other version of **LECA** pebbles for your media bed. In creating your own little universe—a living ecosystem—so many things can go wrong, killing your fish and then your plants. I heartily recommend staying with the tried and true on your first go round.
5. You need to purchase an **aeration pump** for the fish tank. Remember that your fish need oxygen.
1. You need to purchase a small **sump pump** to move your water. I've gone into a lot of detail on

AQUAPONICS GARDENING

this in the glossary, because this is the key to your new ecosystem. If you fail to circulate the water, your grow medium doesn't flourish with bacteria, your ammonia never breaks down, and your plants end up living in an arid wasteland without fertilizer. You need a reliable sump pump.
2. Tubing for circulating the water as it is pumped.
3. PVC pipe, the length determined by the project width and height.
4. Gravel. Expect to purchase 2.5 pounds for each five gallons of water.
5. A drill with three different sizes of bits: ½", ¼", and 3/16".
6. Electrical tape
7. Scissors
8. Fish
9. The planting receptacles for growing your vegetables, seeds and/or plants.

Many of the basic supplies remain the same as for the scrounger, but what you do with them is as different as donkeys and zebras. You're going to create a wowser of a system.

The Engineer's DIY Aquaponic Garden

Some of the basic components will remain the same. For those of you who skipped over the scrounger's detailed instructions, knowing right away you wanted a more tech-savvy kind of system, let's get to it.

1. Set up your fish tank. If your tank doesn't stand on the floor, it needs a sturdy base. If you are using a wooden crate, put in a durable pond liner. I recommend plastic over a glass aquarium, simply by virtue of weight. Here's the thing: at some point you're going to say, "I think it needs to be shifted just two inches to the left." A glass aquarium is heavy and prone to breakage when dropped. Trust me on this.
2. Wash your gravel and line the bottom of the tank.
3. Install PVC pipes for carrying your water to the plant bed(s), and drill holes or water to get into it at various levels. Be sure it's long enough to attach to the growing medium, so water gets injected into the LECA pebbles.
4. Insert your sump pump close to the PVC pipe. Some go so far as to run the hose directly into it, but I don't recommend doing so. You want more of a trickle of constantly flowing water than a river coursing through your system. Give your bacteria a healthy climate and don't wash them away. A **wicking system** will not work for an engineering marvel like this.
5. Fill your aquarium with the desired level of water.

AQUAPONICS GARDENING

6. Attach you aerator if it isn't submersible, or add it to the bottom if it is meant to be inside of the tank.
7. Measure your water temperature and pH level. I recommend using a spiral notebook with columns drawn for recording your daily readings. It's helpful at the outset to track your progress. Leave space on the side of each line to note changes you've made so that you can make correlations and draw correct conclusions on how your system is affected by each change. Your analytical mind will marvel over all of these details and how each affects the others. You should be in your glory here.
8. Welcome your fish. Just starting out, expect to have one fish per plant per 10 gallons of water. As your system becomes more efficient, you can expand and play with these numbers.
9. Place your growing bed above the height of the tank. Your first PVC pipe needs to be attached to the growing bed, and you'll need a second pipe returning water to the aquarium. You'll replicate this step if you are installing more than one grow bed.
10. Figure out how, where, or if you need to install **grow lights**. This is an engineer's nirvana. Remember these kinds of light generate heat that will affect water temperature, bacteria

cultivation, and plant growth. Look for an energy-saving model.

11. Whatever kind of receptacle you're growing your plants within, fill it with the soaked LECA pellets or Hydroton. Allow time for all of the pebbles to settle into the base without floating to the surface. You don't want to clog your pump with pebbles getting sucked into the hose and getting lodged in a delicate mechanism. Take your time in this step to evaluate your water and have it ready to welcome your plants. Rushing may result in plants that fail to thrive.

12. Figure out the best housing for your plants. Your goal is getting roots into the nutrient film. There are multiple ways to accomplish this objective, but I favor attaching a 2-3 or 4-way fitting to the ascending pipe, then running lengths of PVC pipe across the top of the tank. Drill holes into the pipes and secure the nets. Use another multi connector to bring the rows of plants to the descending PVC pipe. Now, this is a system every engineering heart will rhapsodize over. It's clean. It looks nice. It's efficient.

13. Add plants obtained from a local nursery or grown from your windowsill. Wash the dirt out of the roots, and set them gently into the nets.

Are you ready for pictures? Here's one of my favorites, a series of channels with lots of space for plants, a streamlined design, and convenience at its core.

AQUAPONICS GARDENING

Look at the way you can expand your system as you get the hang of the process. This commercial application doesn't have to be so massive. You could accomplish the same thing on a more moderate scale. The key in all of these illustrations is in maximizing your gardening space, while that engineering mind does its thing.

The wonderful thing about aquaponics is its versatility. If you've been the reader who pored over the glossary and kept digging for more information, you want a tech-savvy kind of system. Design what makes you happy.

Chapter Summary

Designing and building a tech-savvy kind of aquaponic garden requires some of the same tools and concepts, but it's going to appeal to a certain kind of do it yourself genius.

- If you have the engineering mind, banish the impatient and the artistic from your workshop.
- Be patient. It will take longer than you want, but it's going to be a great system.

In the next chapter, you will learn all about maximizing your growing potential as you reach for the sky. Read on.

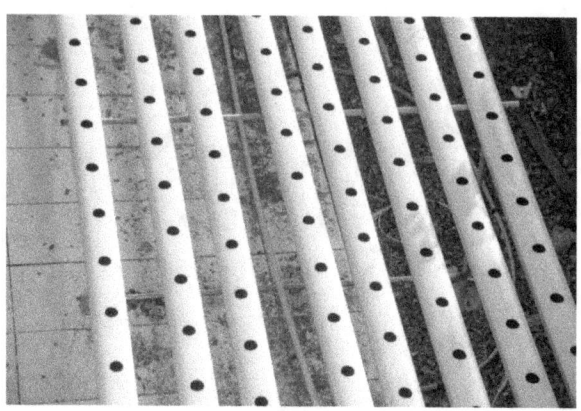

AQUAPONICS GARDENING

AQUAPONICS GARDENING

CHAPTER SEVEN

SETTING UP A TOWERING AQUAPONIC GARDEN

Napoleon's Favorite Option

The idea of growing vertically appeals to me. It takes less space, it's riveting in commanding attention, eliciting a lot of "oohs" and "ahs." It is also more expensive. Don't tune me out. I have my ways, and will help you streamline the process to make it as economical as possible. You may have read the prior two chapters and just not fallen in love with any of the systems outlined. I'm including full instructions here, so you don't have to run back and forth between chapters when you get ready to create your masterpiece. If you're still waiting for the lightning bolt to hit, this may be what you're looking for!

Some of you want the unicorn of all systems, and the tower of gardens is impressive. This will not be a cheap endeavor, and you may still be building it yourself with plans, but what you're creating is more than food for the winter. It's a work of art. It will help if you have construction experience and if you have an engineering mind. Count on learning a lot and *really do your homework ahead of time.*

This system will take time to build, cost more in supplies ,and reap four or five times the amount of produce. Most of the people I know who have creating a towering aquaponic garden, first enjoyed small countertop versions, got their feet wet so to speak, and then built their masterpiece. It is well worth the effort, but this may be your second endeavor, not your first. Your list of supplies will look much like the lists for the scrounger and the engineer with some notable differences. I'm going to describe one way to construct a towering garden, but you'll see pictures and soon realize that there are a dozen ways you can do this.

1. Find or purchase your fish tank. This is your bottom tank. Make sure it's large enough for all of your water needs. Because you're installing multiple growing beds, this is going to take some space, and you'll be ordering more fish to support the additional beds. Depending on how many bedding plants you want, you should probably figure on at least a 100 gallon tank.
2. Order a pH test kit.
3. Order your growing medium. I recommend you spring for either **hydroton** or some other version of **LECA** pebbles for your media bed.

AQUAPONICS GARDENING

Because you're going to transport water to so many growing beds, you need the highest efficiency in your culture. Don't skimp or go cheap in this step.

4. You need to purchase an **aeration pump** for the fish tank. Remember that your fish need oxygen.
5. You need to purchase a **sump pump** to move your water. I've gone into a lot of detail on this in the glossary, because this is the key to your new ecosystem. For a large system, you need one able to move up to 400 gallons of water per hour. This will be your work horse and it needs to be powerful.
6. You need supplies for circulating the water as it is pumped, and in this design, that canal system will function as your bedding containers. You'll spend more on this for towering beds than for either of the other two described projects because you're transporting water further and using it in place of growing containers. I would use PVC piping 3 or 4 inches in diameter. Depending on the number of columns you're designing, you'll need about eight feet per growing column, so do the math and purchase accordingly.
7. Get elbows and T connectors, depending on how many vertical stands you're constructing. I'd plan on four to six. If you're gonna be a bear,

AQUAPONICS GARDENING

be a grizzly. Build a deluxe system that will meet your growing needs.

8. Purchase hoses or tubes for pumping water to the top of each of the vertical towers.
9. Gravel. Expect to purchase 2.5 pounds for every five gallons of water.
10. Saw horses or a workbench.
11. A hack saw, gloves, and safety glasses for cutting the PVC pipes. You'll probably need sandpaper to smooth those cuts.
12. A heat gun or small torch.
13. A spoon or dowel for fashioning your planting holes.
14. A bucket, cold water, and some rags for cooling the plastic once it's hot.
15. You'll need silicone sealant for attaching those end caps without leakage.
16. An adjustable wrench and two adjustable clamps.
17. A drill with different sizes of bits: ½", ⅞".
18. Fish
19. Plants

I'm not gonna lie. A vertical system is more challenging. Many deluxe kits offer growing towers, especially for hydroponic gardening. If you build one, you'll need to engineer the placement of pipes from a fish tank and then upward to each bed, as well as back down for recycling your water. Why would you go to all this extra trouble and expense? For one thing, you can

AQUAPONICS GARDENING

stack up more growing beds in the same square area with corresponding yields of produce. You will harvest continually, as you can always have a bed of seedlings, a bed of half mature produce, and a bed of veggies ready to pick and put on the table. A towering system is easy on your back with less bending over. It's an easier system to design, since your tubes are traveling up and then down, usually in a straight line. When you construct your first bed, you'll just replicate those steps for each of the beds in your blueprint. Lastly, this is a very flexible system and great for urban settings.

Look at some of these beauties! This system of tiered bins is functional and still pleasing to the eyes. This combines the practicality of the scrounger with the heart of the Napoleonic for a very pleasing combination of towering practicality within anyone's budget. This version incorporates warm wood tones for a craftsman's tower of vegetables.

Let's look at the steps involved in constructing *your* work of art. Because this system utilizes PVC pipe for your growing beds, it is clean and tailored, less messy, and easier to manage.

1. Set up your fish tank with a sturdy base. My suggestion is that it stand below window height, both to discourage the growth of algae and to allow as much space as possible for your towering garden.

2. Wash gravel and put it into place.
3. Add the sump pump, and attach an aerator to either the outside of the tank or at the bottom if it is submersible.
4. Now you need to construct your tower. You'll be laying it out on the ground to construct it before you lift it vertically, so pick a good spot as close to its future home as possible.
5. Begin by building a frame for the tower, allowing you to attach each growing tube of plants.
6. Cut your vertical piping. The height will be determined by how tall you want it, and you'll be cutting one length for each tower you want in your garden.
7. You'll need to drill and fashion growing receptacles in each of the vertical pipes. One way is to cut a slit into the pipe, heat with a torch, and then press the soft plastic downward into a lip that will hold your plant. Remember, you can plant all the way around your tube, so dream big and make a lot of plant openings.
8. Drill multiple holes into the end caps and attach them to the base of each grow tube. These allow for drainage back into your fish tank, and you don't want a small pond to develop at the base of the tube, so drill multiple holes.
9. You'll need a horizontal base at the bottom, just above the fish tank for attaching your vertical pipes. You'll also need an identical base at the

top to anchor your pipes in another place. Use stainless steel screws, nuts and bolts to prevent corrosion.

10. Fill each pipe with your growing medium. Be sure it doesn't spill out of your pipe lips and into the fish tank.
11. Run water supply tubing or hosing, one for each growing pipe, up your structure. Work the end of each hose into the top of each of the PVC pipes filled with growth medium. It will trickle down and back into your fish tank at the bottom.
12. Add your fish and let your water world do its magic. Keep track of your readings, and when everything is stable, add your plants.

Chapter Summary

Designing and building a tower garden combines all the ingenuity of a scrounger, all the tech savvy creativity of an engineer, and all of the imagination of an artist. It is a blend especially for those with less space, who can build upward more easily than outward. These designs are eye catchers and show stoppers, so they are well worth the effort.

- Begin by looking at a lot of pictures to stimulate your imagination.
- Read and understand the instructions above. Many of the principles remain the same in every tower garden.
- Get ready to be the envy of your friends and neighbors. Your garden will be epic.

In the next chapter, you will learn how to be humble. Buy a kit. Take time for a siesta and get some help. It's okay. As a matter of fact, it's a great idea for beginners.

AQUAPONICS GARDENING

CHAPTER EIGHT

SETTING UP THE EASIEST AQUAPONIC GARDEN

If You Want a Kit, For Goodness Sake, Get One!

Some of you looked at the last three chapters and your eyes glazed over. There's no shame in admitting it. You just like to learn by doing, and you feel more comfortable starting with a kit for guaranteed success. I felt much the same way when I started out.

Kits are a great way to break into this world, where one little mishap can kill your fish and sets off a chain reaction, killing your plants as well. There's nothing easier than reading the book and then enlisting the best minds on the planet to create your system for you. In this age of specialization, it's a smart way to dip your toe into the exacting world of aquaponic gardening.

Let's begin by getting some perspective on what's out there. Let's say money is no object. If you've got the space and the money, this deluxe model is like the cadillac of all kits. Let's look at something a bit more modest: This is smaller, but I like its streamlined design and ease of maintenance. Kits vary from the small, to the countertop, to the grandiose, and you get to choose depending on what your budget and your circumstances dictate.

Now, it's time to get down to shopping. Seriously. What should you look for when perusing the internet for kits? Size, for one thing. Will it fit into your space and will it grow the volume of vegetables you're wanting? Nothing is worse than buyer's remorse, spending big bucks on a kit and then realizing it's just not what you wanted. The old theory of spending as long researching as it took you to earn that price tag is particularly sage advice here.

Look at one of the detailed sets of DIY tools and be sure to compare it to other kits as you narrow down your options. Is the kit of your choice complete? Some are less in price, but you have to buy all of the extras, which add up. And heaven help us if you get to a certain stage in the process and then realize you don't have some indispensable part and it will be a week before you get it. Frustration is a killer. One more time. Do your homework.

Think about how easy it will be to clean and maintain the kit. I shake my head at some designs, thinking I'd almost prefer pitching it to cleaning it. Was it designed for a one and done kind of garden? That's not what I have in mind.

Don't forget to check on its safety, using food-grade materials. Some cheap kits don't belong in your home, and the chemicals leached from them don't belong in our bodies.

Look for dealers with experience in building several models. Those models all represent time in the field, and time equals experience. If you have your heart set on a small company with one aquaponic gardening kit, look at it critically and read the reviews.

One small end company is Aquasprouts, with a lot of instruction and supplies for you to begin your search for just the right option. It has earned good reviews, is economical, and a great beginner's garden. It's just too small for my family.

At the other end of the spectrum is the Brio company with two options to consider. It's going to cost you some money. You're going to feel like it's a lot of money, but hold onto your hat. In the world of kits, it's not the most expensive out there.

My favorite is a scalable kit that allows you to choose the size you need. This company carries indoor and outdoor systems, with several models to study. Each of those models translates into time and experience. This company has had time to work out the wrinkles and offers a solid product. This is even more expensive than the gorgeous Brio model, but you get a whole lot more growing power for your money.

Let's say money is no object. If you've got the space and the money, this deluxe model is like the cadillac of all kits. Let's look at something a bit more modest: this is smaller, but I like its streamlined design and ease of maintenance. Kits vary from the small, to the countertop, to the grandiose, and you get to choose what your budget and your circumstances dictate.

My personal fave: I love Murray Hallam's Indy 11.5 system as a cross between a kit and a DIY system, providing the best of both worlds. It is expertly designed and includes 60 pages of full color instructions. You do have to buy the building supplies, but the homework has been done for you. The design is eight years old, and it's a proven commodity. In fact, I'm thinking it may be my next outdoor venture.

What I love most about the kit concept is the way it helps the procrastinator in all of us. Yes, we want an aquaponic garden. Um, yes, we want it with all the bells and whistles. Right now is not a good time, there's too much going on to dig in and design one. Wait! A kit? I can do this over a weekend? Hell, yeah! See how much easier it is to make it happen? This is the answer for all of you wannabes who never seem able to make it happen...life just gets in the way. This is for you!

AQUAPONICS GARDENING

Chapter Summary

A kit is valuable when you don't want to reinvent the wheel. You enjoy building on the brains and tips of pioneers in the field, and end up with a highly-prized aquaponic garden in the process. A kit is valuable when:

- You carefully research the marketplace for the design that is best for your situation.
- You are good at following directions, but lack in personal experience or imagination.
- You like convenience and don't mind paying for it.

In the next chapter, you will learn how to take your aquarium and create the right environment for growing healthy fish. It's all about creating a delicate balance between two toxic extremes.

CHAPTER NINE

WHAT'S IN YOUR WATER?

(MORE THAN YOU EVER WANTED TO KNOW ABOUT PH)

You're about to enter into the most critical phase of aquaponic gardening: adjusting your water so that it welcomes fish and produces the perfect stew for plant growth. We've already covered the basics in the cycle of aquaponic life: fish produce waste. The waste clings to inorganic matter (clay pebbles), where colonies of bacteria break down the waste into nitrates the plants can digest. The plants absorb the nutrient laden stew and return it to the fish as clean, wholesome water.

I know that sounds easy, but the truth of the matter is that it's not. You need to create just the right watery stew for optimal fish growth that becomes the right watery stew for plant growth. That involves the level of oxygen, the temperature of the water, and the right degree of acidity. Of these three, acidity is the key factor.

Strap on your seatbelt, because you're about to learn more than you ever wanted to know about **pH balance**. I'm going to offer you a primer in this chapter, and a lot more information in the glossary, complete with links in case you want to delve into the subject further.

First, the basic definition and its explanation. In all of life, there exists a delicate balance of positivity and negativity. Just as in the building blocks of nature, elements present within a sphere of a positive nucleus, jam packed with protons and neutrons and orbiting negative electrons. They are happiest when perfectly balanced in a neutral state. In a chemical reaction, the electrons shift. Think of a parking lot with cars parked in all of the parking stalls. A whistle blows, and every driver races around the lot to park his car in a different stall. In the process, these elements exchange electrons, each attracting or losing electrons, collecting different configurations, and thus creating compounds. Hydrogen and oxygen become gaseous or liquid water, its chemical composition being two parts hydrogen and one part oxygen (H_2O).

Their combination into water creates a stable substance with a perfect balance between positivity and negativity. If you possessed super powers and could look down to see what is happening at the most basic level, you'd see a chemical reaction in which hydrogen was stripped of its electron, making it positively charged. Oxygen was stripped of two electrons, making it negatively charged. They combine in such a way that the extra electrons in the two hydrogen atoms join the vacant parking stalls in the oxygen atom, and suddenly, both have reached a perfect state of neutrality.

This replay of trading electrons and forming new substances goes on all day long in your body in the millions of exchanges regulating the transmission of thought at each synapse, as well as the charging and recharging of each heartbeat. It happens automatically without any effort on your part, and until right now, you may not have even been cognisant of the miracle of life taking place inside of you.

The study of this perfect body stew is called **homeostasis**. That's a fancy word that means keeping the body primed at just the right amount of acidity so these millions of chemical reactions take place. Your body likes a pH of 7.35 to 7.45. Your arterial blood is normal at 7.40. That's a very narrow range for supporting life, but your body maintains it through the transfer of electrically charged elements of calcium, sodium, carbon, and potassium, to name a few.

The measure of acidity or alkalinity is done through measuring the pH. It ranges in a scale from 1 to

14. A lower pH means that your measured substance is more acidic. A higher pH means that your measured substance is more alkaline. Let's look at that water molecule we created at the beginning of the chapter. When water rains down upon us, it is neutrally charged at 7.0. When chemicals get dissolved into the water, its balance shifts.

Acidic substances donate electrons to become negatively charged, and in the process, combine with positively charged substances to create another neutral compound. Everything you see taking place around you depends upon these teeny tiny chemical reactions, moving and parking electrons, changing parking stalls, and always looking for just the right place to land.

When you read the next chapter, you'll be analyzing what kind of watery stew each fish likes. Some live within a very narrow sphere, like your body, and some tolerate wide fluctuations in the acidity versus alkalinity of their watery home. It's going to be your job to create that delicate pH balance your fish like, so just how do you do that?

Your first step will be measuring your aquarium pH. You'll use a kit with litmus paper strips. Dip one into the water and see it turn a color representing its place in the scale of measured acidity or alkalinity printed on the side of the jar containing the litmus strips. It won't matter if you're color blind, because you'll still see some hue in the scale and still be comparing your strip to whatever that color looks like to you.

Most fish will tolerate the water you put into the tank. However, that water won't stay at the neutral pH after the fish begin to inhabit their new home. As they expel waste, they add ammonia (NH_3) into the water. This is a charged compound, making the water acidic. If that waste builds up, you'll begin to smell ammonia, and if it continues to increase, it will reach a toxic level for your fish, preventing the flow of oxygen into their gills, effectively asphyxiating or drowning them. In a normal aquarium you'd be changing the water to make it neutral once again.

That's a different kind of exercise when you have a 50, 100, or 500 gallon tank of water. This is where your clay pebbles come into play. They house bacteria that cause important chemical reactions. One type of bacteria (nitrosomonas) will change the NH_3 to NO_2 (a nitrite), and another bacteria (nitrobacter) will take the nitrite and change it into NO_3 (a nitrate). This nitrate is just what your plants need to grow, and they'll absorb it into their roots. You can't effectively add plants until these nitrates are present in the water, and it can take up to thirty days to get a healthy environment up and running.

★ The **nitrogen cycle** is the process of keeping your aquaponic garden running like the rest of the universe, in a constant recycling of nutrients.

AQUAPONICS GARDENING

Here's the normal progression you'll see when you add your fish to the water. First, you'll record an increase in acidity, as your fish excrete waste into the water. Then, you'll see a shift, as the bacteria kick in and start doing their magic. That's when you may introduce plants, which will cleanse the water as they absorb these nitrates.

In the process of it all, you'll need to measure your water's acidity as well as levels of nitrites and nitrates, every couple of days to be sure the optimal balance is being maintained. If it becomes too acidic, you'll need to exchange water or lessen the waste by feeding your fish less.

Nitrates, however, are just one measurement involved in maintaining a healthy aquaponic garden. Just as important is the regulation of water temperature. Your fish will be cold-blooded. Why does that matter? They cannot generate body heat and it falls upon you to regulate the water to their comfort and health. When a child's temperature rises just three degrees, we become concerned over the fever and work at reducing his/her temperature. Your fish will suffer similarly when you're water temperature fluctuates wildly.

★ Aim for no more than three degrees of change within a given twenty-four hour period.

Factors affecting your tank water temperature include your heat source, your climate, and how warm or cool your keep your home (if indoors), the amount of piping your water travels through, how you place your tanks, your growing bed, and whether or not you insulate parts of your system. Of course, you want to reduce your energy consumption and thereby reduce your cost of operation. For this, one of the simplest things you can do is to insulate your tanks, grow bed, and pipes. All of this requires a willingness to set up your tanks and to monitor your conditions before investing in either fish or plants.

You also need to monitor the oxygenation of your water. We've covered getting an aerator to add oxygen, but how do you know if you have the amount of fish you need? The level of dissolved oxygen directly affects your fish growth, and the level of nitrifying bacteria for converting waste into fertilizer. Your goal is 100% oxygen saturation, and to do that you must mimic Mother Nature. Streams and rivers remain oxygenated by air bubbles trapped in molecules of water during rainfall. They dissolve into the water and increase the oxygen level. In your aquarium, you mimic this process through the use of an **aeration pump**.

All of this discussion points to getting a good kit for measuring your water and for keeping records. **Water testing kits** come in many different forms, some more expensive than others:

1. The handiest and cheapest form are dry test strips. The reagents are already applied and the

color changes pinpoint measured levels, comparing them to the guide on the jar.
2. Liquid test kits require you to take samples of your tank water, add reagents, and then read the color after some time has elapsed. These are very accurate.
3. The most expensive form is a photometer, requiring frequent calibration.

Look at the links in your glossary and find one that meets your needs. Don't be scared by the prices you see when you start shopping for a kit. Yes, they are expensive, but think about how long they last. Each kit has a lot numbers printed on it, and usually the last four digits are the month and year it was manufactured. You'll want to keep track of that number, because your equipment lasts a long time.

AQUAPONICS GARDENING

Chapter Summary

Maintain the proper level of acidity or alkalinity in your water by:

- Measuring your water pH level several times each week.
- Lower the acidity by exchanging water in the tank.
- Lower the acidity by feeding your fish less.
- Lower the acidity by introducing plants.

In the next chapter, you will learn about which fish you want to invite to your new fishy home.

PART III

FILLING YOUR AQUAPONIC SYSTEM WITH LIFE

CHAPTER TEN

WHAT'S ON THE MENU?

You already know your fish tank can become a home to everything from ornamental koi to cod, but you have to decide on which fish to purchase. This chapter is devoted to looking at some of your choices and the types of factors that will influence your decision. Among your most basic considerations are cost, how quickly they reproduce, and your growing conditions.

Ornamental Fish—Koi and Goldfish

These lovelies are not edible, but they are certainly good looking.

Koi can live in temperatures ranging from 59 to 77 degrees Fahrenheit, requiring a pH of 7 to 8. They are hardy, easy keepers, and long living. At maximum size, they can grow to two feet over thirty years.

Goldfish come in two varieties, denoted by their tails. The single tail is more aggressive than the double-tailed variety, and breeders don't recommend putting both in the same tank. They love a temperature between 78 and 82 degrees Fahrenheit, pH 6 to 8. They are hardy and can reach a pound in size within one year.

Comet goldfish are American-bred with deeply forked tails. They come in several colors and can grow to twelve inches in length over 10 or 15 years.

Shunbunkin goldfish originate from Japan. They are very attractive and can grow to over 15 inches in length.

The lion head goldfish are very popular, because of their distinctive heads and various colorings. They live up to 15 years, but seldom grow more than 6 inches long. When we look at the number of fish you must carry, keep that smaller size in mind.

Fantail goldfish are extremely hardy and great for beginners. They have a distinctively short, egg-shaped body with a wide head. They may grow up to 10 inches in length over 15 years.

Other ornamentals, such as tetras and guppies are less hardy and more demanding. Also, bear in mind a few caveats. Many ornamentals have been treated with antibiotics or other chemicals that are stored in their flesh. Yes, they are bringing those to your aquaponic garden. Ornamentals have also been known to carry TB, worms, and other parasites.

AQUAPONICS GARDENING

Tilapia

If you're ready to dive in with fish you'll eventually be eating for dinner, one of the most common is tilapia. Did you know there are three species of tilapia? Neither did I. There are white, gold, and blue tilapia.

The gold tilapia is a tough species, and can tolerate water temperatures anywhere between 75 and 98 degrees Fahrenheit, and need a pH of 6.5 to 9. They can survive poor water quality, pollution, and low levels of oxygenated water. They are also the most disease resistant. The blue tilapia grows much more slowly, taking as long as 3 years to reach 2 to 4 pounds. The white tilapia is an offshoot of the blue species, but it grows as fast as the gold and survives temperatures as low as 50 degrees Fahrenheit.

If you're wanting a faster turnover from fish to vegetables on the table, the white is the better choice. About this point you should be wondering what these fish eat. Off the shores of Hawaii, they would eat algae and tiny one-celled organisms, but you're going to be eliminating algae from your tank. That means you need to buy an organic source of **fish food.** Some cheaper versions will be made from fish waste, crushed bones, and other byproducts, but these are not good for your fish, especially if you plan on harvesting them for table consumption.

★ Feed your fish well, and they can grow to full size in as little as eight months. Feed them poorly, and they may never gain a pound.

Full grown tilapia are a delicious addition to your dinner table. To harvest them, it is recommended that you put them into a separate tank for three to five days, withholding all food, thus cleansing the digestive tract.

How large a tank do you need to grow tilapia? A fully grown fish needs three gallons of water. That equals one fish per every 3 to 6 gallons of water. Let's look at those figures realistically. If you are growing tilapia, you are looking at a tank holding about 130 gallons, able to handle 20 to 40 fully grown tilapia.

To summarize, tilapia are the most popular of the large fish in aquaponic gardens, because of their relatively fast rate of growth, hardiness, and mild flavor. Expect to spend money on organic food and a water heater, and make sure you have a large tank.

Pacu

This fish comes from a region with jungles and rainforests, so it requires warm water (between 75-88 degrees Fahrenheit), pH 6.5 to 7.5. They do not live amicably with other fish, so even though they don't feed off them, refrain from putting them together. Also pay attention to its full grown size: 3½ feet long and 88 pounds. Do I need to warn you about having a very large system?

Catfish

These are actually great fish for your aquaponic garden. They grow to full size within one year and are known for their hardiness when a tank's system gets polluted. In addition, they do well in temperatures between 75 and 86 degrees Fahrenheit, pH 7 to 8.5, making them easy keepers. Catfish grow no scales, so plan on skinning them before they hit the pan.

On the plus side, you can add some variety to your tank, because this is not a territorial species. On the minus side, they need a high protein fish food, so keep that in mind before investing in them. Midway through the year you don't want to suddenly feel like you are spending *way too much* money on fish food and experience buyer's remorse.

Trout

Prized by gourmands, this is a fun breed to grow. They tolerate colder water, so be sure you want to grow vegetables that will also tolerate cooler water, around 45 to 65 degrees Fahrenheit, pH 6.5 to 8. They grow slowly and enjoy an eclectic palate of fish, insects, and small invertebrates. Those all sound attractive until you look at the other side of the coin.

These fish don't play well with other species. Be sure you only want trout. They need a lot of space and they grow slowly. They also require higher levels of oxygenated water (a minimum of 10 mg/min), so plan on getting a high quality aerator for your tank.

Carp

These fish are popular in Asia, but not so much in most Western cultures. As a matter of fact, in the United States, where they are considered pests, you may get fined for having them. Surprisingly, the goldfish is a smaller and distant relative to the carp, a testament to the species' versatility.

Cod

If you don't want to heat your water, the murray cod is an excellent choice, as it withstands a range of 46 to 75 degrees Fahrenheit, pH 7 to 8. It grows to an adult weight of 1 pound in 12 to 18 months. They make great friends for different kinds of perch, but realize they are omnivorous and will eat smaller fish, even resorting to attacking one another if you neglect to feed them enough. These fish enjoy a very long lifespan of up to 15 years, so if you don't plan on harvesting them for the table, they make a great investment in your aquaponic garden.

Jade Perch

A native of Australia, this fish tolerates water temperatures of 60 to 85 degrees Fahrenheit, pH 6.5-8.5. One thing that endears it to aquaponic gardeners is its taste for vegetables and vegetable waste, eating scraps normally composted. It will grow to one pound in twelve months. This is an excellent fish for the table, as it is high in omega-3 fatty acids.

Bass

American fishermen prize bass, and enjoy their mild taste. They tolerate water temperatures of 65 to 80 degrees Fahrenheit, pH 7.2 to 8, and reach maturing in one year. There are several kinds: large-mouth, smallmouth hybrid striped, and white bass. If you catch them from a local pond or lake, you can transplant them into your aquaponic garden, eliminating the cost of buying them.

Barramundi

A native of Asia, plan on keeping water temperature higher for this breed of fish: 71 to 80 degrees Fahrenheit. They eat a lot, so of course there will be a lot of waste, which can put your system out of whack. The adult fish will eat the fingerlings, so don't plan on keeping breeding fish together.

This is a fast-growing fish, but experts suggest it's not the best fish for beginners. Take their advice.

Crappie

This species comes is different sizes and colorings. They take two years to grow to a full size of one 1 pound, so don't expect a fast turnaround. They tolerate water between 60 to 75 degrees Fahrenheit, pH 6.5 to 8.2, making them quite hardy. They will be happier living with their own kind, and so will you.

Blue Gill

Native to North America, these are common in the United States. You will find them easy to catch and transfer to your aquaponic garden. They like their water between 70 and 75 degrees, a narrow range to manage, and like a pH of 7 to 9. It makes many friends in the fish family and will reach table size in one year.

Freshwater Prawns and Shrimp

These are very profitable fish to raise and sell as part of your aquaponic garden, as they are the number one source of seafood consumed worldwide. They tolerate water temperatures between 57 and 84 degrees Fahrenheit, pH 6.5 to 8, and may be harvested within 3 to 6 months. They don't like change, so stabilize your tank before obtaining them.

Salmon

These are delicious fish, but very large, needing very large tanks. They like a temperature of 55 to 65

AQUAPONICS GARDENING

degrees Fahrenheit, pH 7 to 8. It takes 2 years to grow one to full size. They are tolerant of cool conditions, but realize that you can't manage them out of doors if you live in a temperate climate with hot summers. They are not resistant to disease and require more food per pound than all other fish used in aquaponic gardening.

Chapter Summary

In this chapter, we reviewed the many types of fish available for aquaponic gardening. Choice of which fish you want to employ in stocking your tank rests on variables such as size, cost, ability to get along with friends, and life requirements. Choosing to harvest your fish requires setting up a breeding tank to ensure you always have a supply of new fish coming on to replace the ones you harvest. There is a fish for every aquaponic enthusiast:

- ornamental fish
- tilapia
- pacu
- catfish
- trout
- carp
- cod
- Jade perch
- bass
- barramundi
- crappie

AQUAPONICS GARDENING

- blue gill
- freshwater lobster or shrimp
- salmon

In the next chapter, you will learn about the vegetables you may want to grow in your aquaponic garden.

CHAPTER ELEVEN

FOR A SMALL SYSTEM, GROW A LETTUCE BOWL

Because we wanted a small indoor system where we could enjoy the fish and easily harvest our produce, I first opted for growing a medley of veggies great for a lettuce bowl. I cannot remember making salads with just one kind of lettuce, so for me, it's always about the blend of flavors and colors. Adding peppers, tomatoes, cucumbers, chickpeas, hard boiled egg quarters, strips of smoked cheese, nuts, and fruits always takes a back seat to a great bed of greens.

For a home garden, I choose different greens from a commercial perspective—I use larger leaf lettuce over microgreens. When I mix up a huge salad bowl, I'm normally feeding 12 to 16 people. We entertain a lot, so sometimes I'm feeding 25 or 30. For those numbers, I'm more interested in how much salad I'm making rather than whether or not gourmands are impressed with those tiny, highly valued microgreens. So, unless it's just the two of you, or your family picks at salads (so why are you growing greens?) I recommend the following:

I always grow two types of lettuce. The green varieties vary based on my mood when I plant, but my favorites are romaine and black seeded Simpson. In addition, I always grow a ruby lettuce variety. It's tangier, so it adds both color and bite to the salad bowl.

Also, I always grow spinach as one addition to the salad bowl. Harvest the leaves when they are small for a sweet, delicate flavor. Pinch off any tendency to bolt.

★ Freeze the seeds for a day before planting them to hasten the germination process.

Kale is an important staple in our household. I often add it to salads, but I also love to wash the leaves and freeze it. I don't blanch it. I just wash and dry the leaves, stuff them in freezer bags, and toss them into the upright. When I make soups or stews during the winter, I take a bag out, crush up all the leaves and pour them in for extra vitamins, nice color and definition, with a bit of a punch. When it comes to cooking fresh kale, my family prefers to ignore anything healthy. They like for me to fry up a mess of bacon. Then saute in some minced garlic, add the greens, wilt it all, and top it with the bacon. (Don't yell at me. They're eating greens!)

If I grow any microgreens for my table, it's a plant or two of arugula (a little goes a long way) and a few watercress. In Victorian days, watercress sandwiches were quite a delicacy, but in my family, not so much. We like it in salads, and like the crinkly-edged leaves the best.

Pak choi is another vegetable many opt to grow, though it isn't one of my regulars. It is a form of Chinese cabbage and you'll find it in several dishes at Chinese restaurants. You'll find it very suitable for your aquaponic garden because of its compact growth and densely green, nutritious leaves. It can grow in partial shade and in containers, making it a great choice for a lettuce bowl over a vegetable plate.

Herbs earn a prominent place in my indoor garden. Of course, I don't grow all of the following all of the time, but my top choices are Italian parsley, rosemary, and mint. Let me give you a few words about each one.

Italian parsley is a wonderful garnish for spaghetti and lasagna, or any form of pasta. It tastes mild and the color, sprinkled over the top, earn rave reviews before anyone takes that first bite. It never disappoints.

I like to grow basil and use it in soups and stews. I also like to harvest it to make pesto. I put the pesto into small ice cube tray compartments, freeze it, and then put them into little baggies in the freezer. It's easy to extract a small amount of pesto to garnish any dish. I've added an easy, no fuss pesto recipe to a later chapter, in case you're new to it.

Thyme is wonderful on poultry. No turkey gets roasted at our house without two or three handfuls of thyme to season both the meat and the stock. If it matures before Thanksgiving, I simply harvest the plant, tie it up by the kitchen window to let it dry, and break off what I want when it's time to use it.

I use mint in the summer for tea, lemonade, and strawberry salads, but I never want to grow it out of doors. It's a highly invasive plant, so an aquaponic garden is the perfect place to contain its wandering ways.

Chives are wonderful to have on hand with baked potatoes. A baked potato bar is a favorite meal in our household, and everyone loves to sprinkle snipped chives over their sour cream—as well as cheese, bacon, broccoli, and a medley of wonderful toppings.

Sage assumes a huge role in our household. Besides offering a savory twist to stews and dressing mixes, my family loves it crushed into their biscuits for a Saturday morning biscuits and gravy feast.

I only grow a few sprigs of rosemary. I love it on meatloaf, but it's not high on my list of stocked staples.

Last, but not least, cilantro is not easy to grow due to its tendency to bolt, but we eat so much Tex-Mex, I have to grow it. The nice thing about growing your own stash is that when you buy a bunch at the market, it has a short shelf life. You'll be able to harvest just the right amount you need for salsa, guacamole, or as a garnish.

AQUAPONICS GARDENING

Chapter Summary

If you have a small aquaponic garden, growing a salad bowl is a wonderful use for your space. You will enjoy the benefits of lovely fish and the fresh veggies that make salads a memory.

- For a home salad, grow several varieties of lettuce and spinach.
- Kale is valuable in smoothies, cooked as a vegetable, or frozen for winter stews.
- Fresh herbs are wonderful as garnishes and flavorings.

In the next chapter, you will learn about vegetables for a larger aquaponic gardening setup.

AQUAPONICS GARDENING

CHAPTER TWELVE

FOR A LARGE SYSTEM, GROW A VEGETABLE PLATE

You don't have to be a vegetarian to love vegetables, and you don't have to grow a wide variety to be a successful gardener. As a matter of fact, in aquaponic gardening, you are well advised to choose carefully those foods you eat the most, and focus on selectively growing a smaller variety of plants.

Some do especially well in your setting, and among those are tomatoes, peppers, cucumbers, beans, squash, peas, broccoli, cauliflower, cabbage, and peppers. As a matter of fact, depending on the size of your fish tank and the size of your growing bed, some are better suited for indoor growth than for outdoor cultivation. Let's go through them.

Tomatoes

This is a mainstay in our household. In the summer in my outdoor garden, I often grow up to 100 plants, just to be sure I have enough to turn into luscious salsa, tomato juice, tomato sauce, spaghetti sauce, and still have plenty to put on the table. You may find the vast numbers of varieties overwhelming, so let's go through the basics.

Whether you have an indoor or an outdoor system, and whether you have space for one, twenty, or fifty plants, you'll still want to look carefully at all the varieties available. If you plan on growing your plants from seeds, look at two great companies. Burpee seed company has been around long enough to win respect nationwide and you can't go wrong with anything you order from them. I prefer Johnny's for their selection of non-GMO and organic offerings.

If you want to plant them in an outdoor garden, start them right after Christmas. I like to have well-developed roots and strong plants to transplant into the garden. I start in plenty of time, using either trays or plug flats. When the plants have true leaves, I flip them out carefully into a larger receptacle and let time do its magic. I plant them in soil and then wash my roots for transplanting them into an aquaponic system.

I like a nice slicer for table use, and Johnny's Big Beef F1 is a great beefeater for BLTs. Since this one is a hybrid (denoted by the F in its title) variety, you can't save and replant the seeds. It ripens in about seventy days, and is resistant to several diseases. I plant the full packet so that I can share seedlings with friends and sell some to recoup my costs.

We eat a lot of cherry tomatoes, and I order Johnny's Supersweet 100 F1. It is known for being prolific and as a sweet snack—a great combination. We like to pop them in our mouths whenever we work in the garden.

Many grow a special variety for tomato paste, but we use whatever I have and just cook them down until they are nice and thick, If you want a specialty tomato just for paste, try Johnny's Amish Paste variety, which is both organic and heirloom. You can save these seeds from one year to the next.

If I don't get my seeds started, I end up getting small, established plants from a local nursery. I fall head over heels for too many varieties, and go home with a medley of Jet Star, Early Girl, Beefeater, and...well, you can see where this is going. By the end of the summer, my plant tags have washed or blown away and I have no idea which plant is which. I'm just plucking and the family is canning like crazy.

You can see why I favor an indoor aquaponic system, growing just what I need for table use. It is so much more manageable, and I end up with tomatoes year round.

Peppers

Peppers are the second villain in my over-burgeoning outdoor garden. I am never content with just a simple bell pepper. Oh no. I have to have two varieties of bell peppers, along with yellow, orange, and red peppers. Then I need several kinds of warm peppers, jalapenos and what not for salsas.

An indoor aquaponic garden usually limits me to one pepper plant, and I pick my favorite. I like Johnny's Gourmet F1 orange bell pepper for salads and for family eating. We slice them into strips to take the place of potato chips, and love their sweet flavor. A close second is their Carmen, an organic F1 corno di Toro Pepper seed. One of our favorite vegetable medleys is green beans sauteed with strips of pepper and craisins. This pairs well in that medley of flavors. (See the recipes in this book!)

Squash

We love zucchini and I like to grow it indoors. Squash bugs destroy plants early in the season, despite multiple efforts to prevent them. We often plant them outdoors after the 4th of July, and the plants survive longer than when planted in the spring, but still fall victim to those sap-sucking borers in the course of time. We relentlessly pick off the pests and feed them to the chickens, but that only delays the process. We maniacally check for eggs deposited underneath the leaves and scrape them off carefully, but we still end up losing our plants, and I hate paying for zucchini at the market when I had it in my garden just a few weeks before hand.

My top choice are the summer squash. You already know I love zucchini, and if you have limited space, one plant can take up three feet as it grows and blossoms. As such, you can probably only have one, so choose wisely.

Cucumbers

I favor an English cuke with an edible skin. I like the long, narrow seedless varieties over the typical fat cucumbers you see in stores. Johnny's Poniente organic F1 is a great choice, as is the Socrates F1. Both are thin-skinned, have excellent flavor, and are disease resistant. Plus, both are great for indoor gardens.

If you grow an upright version and tie up the vines as it grows, it doesn't have to take up a lion's share of your space. I use small trellises so I can spread out its branching growth. I have used garden fencing, but too many cukes ended up growing on the other side of the fence and were hard to pick, so I went back to a more traditional trellis. They make such a lovely sight, dangling there and inviting themselves to lunch.

Beans

An indoor plant is wonderful for table use. I love to pick a few beans and steam them for supper, without having to pick a bushel for canning. Over and over, I think you're seeing the advantage to an aquaponic garden when it comes to growing a vegetable plate. You're looking at quality of produce, not volume.

I still would grow an upright variety of green beans over a bush, just to make it lovely and to save some space, but there are several varieties to choose from. Johnny's Jade is an excellent pole bean with long sweet fruit that presents well in a vegetable plate.

Beans need successive plantings to maintain a consistent harvest, so bear that in mind as you plan out your space. You'll need to start a cycle of plantings, seedlings, transplants and rotate them on a regular basis.

Peas

I admit it. I don't like cooked peas. For me it's a texture thing, because I love to eat them raw in salads and as snacks. Whether you are a pea lover or not, however, peas are great for your garden.

If you are planning a traditional outdoor plot, in addition to your indoor aquaponic garden, peas are your new best friend. The plant can be tilled into your garden to feed it valuable nutrients at the end of the growing season, and you can use your indoor plants to good advantage. My favorite is Johnny's Super Sugar Snap, which is great sauteed with strips of peppers and green beans. They also taste great in salads and in Chinese dishes.

Broccoli

I find broccoli better suited to indoor than outdoor growth, as it often bolts in my garden and proves good for nothing. Johnny's Eastern Magic F1 is my favorite variety. The added benefit of growing it indoors in an aquaponic garden is fewer caterpillars and slugs. You don't have as many hard-to-find pests to remove prior to eating your produce either.

Cauliflower

Have you looked at the price of cauliflower at your local market lately? Because it serves as a low glycemic substitute for potatoes, it has grown in popularity. Growing your own is a great alternative to watching for sales. I'm a bit of a purist, and prefer Johnny's Amazing variety over all of the purple and other unusual types of plants.

Be careful in growing it, as it likes a mild 70 degrees and your fish may find that a little warm. Grow lights add heat and will not be your friend. It is traditionally an early spring or late fall kind of crop, but you can tailor your indoor conditions successfully with a little care.

Cabbage

This is another of my least favorite vegetables in the garden. It is harvested by the head, and deep down inside the plant I find all kinds of worms when I start to clean and separate the leaves. As a result, it is perfect for your aquaponic setting. Just realize that it takes up a fair amount of space and is only good for one harvest.

Chapter Summary

You don't need a huge aquaponic garden to enjoy some of these larger, delectable vegetables all year long. My top pick is the tomato, but you have a lot of options.

- A vegetable plate suggests several kinds of plants. Grow one or two of each.
- Choose those you can grow within your own space confines. You have a lot of choices:
    - Tomatoes
    - Peppers
    - Squash
    - Cucumbers
    - Beans
    - Peas
    - Cauliflower
    - Cabbage

Once you've decided *what* to grow, you have to decide *how to start growing it*. In the next chapter, we'll explore ways to get your garden established.

AQUAPONICS GARDENING

CHAPTER THIRTEEN

HOW DO I START GROWING PLANTS?

By now you're probably rarin to go, but still wondering: "How on earth do I get started?" This is a legitimate question. For those of us who have gardened in the backyard, we know exactly what to do: broadcast some seeds, cover them with soil, keep them moist, and voila! Plants appear.

In an aquaponic garden, things are a little different. I'll go through three ways and leave you to figure out the best option for your situation. Realize there is no one right way.

First of all, you can propagate seedlings as you always have, starting them in potting soil. If you choose this method, pay attention to instructions. Lettuce should be covered with a bare quarter inch of soil. Let your seedlings grow there at least until the second leaves (the true leaves) pop out. Gently lift them from your soil and rinse away any debris that might clog the filters in your tank. Dip the baby roots in a root stimulating powder or solution, and plant it carefully in your growth medium. I would probably opt to leave them longer and make sure they are sturdy before transplanting. *Be careful not to touch the stems in the process.* I've made that mistake and it never ends well.

A second way involves taking cuttings or clonings, and inserting them directly into the growth medium. Basil and mint both do well with this method. General principles include using a very sharp knife and cutting at an angle. Dip the cut end in rooting powder and insert it into the growth medium. Watch for it to take off, and don't get impatient. As long as your leaves haven't wilted and died, there is yet hope.

Some plants can be propagated from their parents. Endive, for example, is easy to do. Cut off the bottom of a head of endive, and put it in water. New plants will grow from the base, and you can transplant these cuttings into your growth medium. I find this more of a conversational oddity than a viable way to grow my veggies. In my experience, the new head of Romaine is smaller and takes up all the growing space of a full-sized plant. Children enjoy watching the process, though, so if you have littles, go for it!

Another popular form, especially for new gardeners, is purchasing starter plants from a local nursery. This is the third way to acquire plants. Before you capitulate and do that, though, give yourself a chance. I like to take a wet paper towel, cast lettuce seed on it, fold it over and stick it in a cool dark place for a few days. When the little darlings germinate, I dip them in a rooting solution and put them in the growth medium.

I'm a diehard seed grower, and it's still my go-to for accumulating plants for any kind of garden. I pore over seed catalogs and order my seeds before Christmas. In January I start them in trays of soil or plug trays. I keep them in the dark until the first leaves appear, and then add grow lights. When the first true leaves appear, the third and fourth leaves on the plant, I transplant them into a place they can call home for a couple months. Pinch back growth to make a bushier plant. Run your hands over your tomato seedlings to encourage stronger stems.

I keep them watered and seldom need to add fertilizer before they are planted or sold. In aquaponic gardening, it is important to have a strong root system before moving them to a grow bed. As before, remember you have to gently wash out the dirt, and you want the roots strong enough to handle a little manipulation.

Some aquaponic growers talk about broadcasting seed directly over the growth medium, and just placing a layer of pebbles on top of the seeds. Personally, I have not done that. It sounds easy, but I'm old school and slightly suspicious.

AQUAPONICS GARDENING

Chapter Summary

Growing your plants is the second half of the aquaponic adventure. It's my favorite part.

- Decide how you want to get or grow your plants. If you are new to gardens, obtaining plants from a nursery is the fastest and easiest route to go.
- Starting your plants from seeds takes time. Don't expect immediate gratification.

In the next chapter, you will learn how to keep all of your hard work alive and growing.

AQUAPONICS GARDENING

CHAPTER FOURTEEN

MAINTENANCE AND PEST PREVENTION

First of all, realize that most of the problems found in traditional gardens will be eliminated without the soil. Why do you think farmers rotated crops for so many years? This is especially true when it comes to growing vegetables.

Cutworms and slugs are disgusting. Period. No longer will you need to sprinkle diatomaceous earth over the soil to discourage mollusks. Fungal and bacterial diseases propagating in the soil will no longer be an issue. (It's helpful to put a paper collar around lettuce seedlings to keep caterpillars at bay, but with aquaponic gardening you don't have to worry about any of that.) Hallelujah!

Now you can stop rejoicing, although you have other things to worry about. Your aquaponic garden is a balancing act. You need a balance between the number of fish you stock, the surface area of your biofilter, and the number of plants you grow. Your success will be determined by how well you regulate that balance and maintain a healthy environment.

Think of your fish on one side of a playground teeter totter. Your plants are on the other. The beam between the two is your biofilter with its bacteria turning ammonia into nitrates. Too little surface area means not enough bacteria, which means not enough fertilizer to grow the plants, leading to ammonia toxicity, killing the fish. On the other hand, if you stock too many fish or feed them too much, your waste may not be handled by the biofilter in place and that can also cause ammonia toxicity. Too many plants and not enough fish means your fish may be fine, but your plants will not flourish. It's a living ecosystem and you're in charge.

Before you freak out, remember: you have measuring devices to keep things under control. You just have to know what your readings mean and how to use them to adjust your system.

Let's talk about three measurements:
- Nitrogen balance: Increased levels of ammonia or nitrite suggest you have a problem with your biofilter. You need increased surface area for culturing bacteria. If your nitrate level is low, you either have too many plants or not enough fish.
- Food balance: The food ratio for leafy vegetables is 40-50 g/m^2/day. Fruiting

vegetables, like tomatoes require 50-80 g/m²/day.

- Health assessments: Each day as you feed your fish and monitor your system, look for the tell tale signs of disease. Dead fish or plants are symptoms of a system out of whack.

One of the issues you need to safeguard against is mold. Let's talk about what mold is and is not. The white calcification you sometimes see on your growth bed is not mold. Green strands are **algae**, not mold. Look up methods to prevent algae formation in the glossary, because this could be a killer for your system as well, though it won't kill your plants or spread the same way as mold.

Mold is an opportunistic pathogen grown from spores. One type is a powdery mildew that will appear on your leaves as white spots. A more serious problem is white mold, which looks fuzzy and can grow to alarming proportions if left unchecked. At first detection, it may look like a harmless speck of white fluff, but it can turn into cankers and destroy the roots of your plant.

Mold develops because of contamination. A spore is introduced into your system. The warm, moist conditions prove favorable to its growth, until it overwhelms your system. Keep a well-ventilated system in place for moving air and don't let stagnant water sit in your trays.

Remove infected leaves immediately. You can wash them off with hydrogen peroxide to help prevent the spread. You can also introduce beneficial bacteria like Bacillus A. One way to eliminate mold is the use of a fungicide. The Serenade garden mold control spray is a broad-spectrum fungicide.

Mold isn't the only thing that will kill your plants, however. There are also a host of pests that may attack your plants. You have an advantage if you grow your plants indoors, but insects always seem to find a way to your garden. Your first defense is a healthy plant. An unstressed plant has high levels of phosphorus in its cells, and that repels some insects. But realize ahead of time that you are putting together an artificial system, and it is vulnerable to damage from insects.

One healthy way to rid your garden of unwanted insects is to capture them using a pheromone trap. They are specific to the insect, so one kind of trap will not fix all kinds of problems. Think of it as a glue trap collecting unwanted guests, only this trap actually attracts them. Be careful in its use. You will need to keep them away from children and pets, and you will need to wash your hands after using them. If the trap is made for outdoor use, don't try to use it indoors. Read all of the product labels before trying to use one.

Another way is to manually remove offending pests. The cabbage white fly lives on the back of leaves. Picking them off will help reduce populations, because they produce 10 to 12 generations a year. You can feed them to your fish, who love a good, high-protein morsel. You can also drop them into a jar of soapy water and flush them away. The key is removing them immediately before they have a chance to reproduce. Another organic spray is BotaniGuard. For whiteflies, spray it directly on the plants or under the leaves. For aphids, spray it into the grow medium. It may take multiple applications to eliminate your pests, and you can use it weekly afterwards to prevent further problems.

Thrips are tiny insects that both suck out plant juices from the leaves, but also carry plant viruses. About as big as a sewing needle is wide, these are hard to see. This will be a bigger issue if your garden is out of doors, as the mature insect winters in plant debris and bark. It lays its eggs in early spring, and can produce up to fifteen generations per year. Thrips will look like little slivers unless you use a magnifying glass, and then be prepared for the shock of seeing a little animal with arms and pincers dining on your leaves. You'll more easily spot their damage in silvery and white speckles on plant leaves. Left untreated, you'll more likely see a virus causing some kind of wilting on your mature plants. You can shake them off, but that may not be aggressive enough if you're looking at an infestation.

AQUAPONICS GARDENING

If your aquaponic garden is outside, get rid of weeds and vegetation that provide a place for them to live. Introduce beneficial insects into your garden, things like pirate bugs, ladybugs or lacewing. Watch your plants and remove diseased leaves. You can use sticky traps to catch them manually. Since you can't employ an insecticide without affecting your fish, consider using a safe product like neem oil to treat them.

Neem oil is a safe and natural deterrent for thrips. It is extracted from the neem tree, grown in India, and contains natural insecticide and antifungal properties. It is often ingested for its medicinal properties, but the EPA deemed it safe for use in farming. There is no warning for residues with repeated application. It can be used on plant leaves without fear of affecting your fish.

All of this is made more difficult due to your ecosystem. You must learn to spot and eliminate pests without poisoning your water. You may also make your own organic spray, but be careful. What you use must be good for fish, as well as for plants. The most natural sprays you can make yourself. Use chile or garlic sprays for sap-sucking insects. For mold or fungus, you can spray a solution of potassium bicarbonate.

Chapter Summary

An aquaponic garden has natural enemies, and they attack at will. From one-celled spores to insects threatening plant annihilation, you must be prepared for the worst.

- Healthy plants are your biggest defense.
- Monitor for problems and be proactive in solving them.
- Be careful not to cause a problem in solving one. Utilize organic fish-friendly methods to discourage unwanted growth.

In the next chapter, you will learn how to take what you've learned and turn it into a business. You've made an investment, let's see a return on it in the form of profits.

CHAPTER FIFTEEN

COMMERCIAL APPLICATIONS OF AQUAPONIC GARDENING

As much as you love organic produce for your own table, don't overlook the possibility of turning a little money—or a lot—in selling what you grow. As a lover of farmer's markets, both as a consumer and as a vendor, there's a whole lot of fulfillment in the process of making money from what you love.

Begin by deciding what you grow best. For us, it was vegetables more than fish. Our setup was too small to efficiently run fish through on a scale large enough to make aquaculture profitable. However, the ability to grow more in a smaller space paid off big time. We focused on lettuce bowl veggies, primarily microgreens.

The next step is finding your market. We harbored fantasies of finding restaurants and grocery stores that would contract with us for regular deliveries of our produce. That did not happen. Agribusinesses already had contracts or provided for their own needs, and breaking into that market while vegetables went bad was not an option.

For us, the farmer's market was the easiest way to get our produce to market. We paid a small amount for a weekly stall, and once shoppers learned what we had, we enjoyed weekly visits from them. We loved it.

Our best crop came from leafy greens, specifically **microgreens,** used in salads. We started with mesclun, a salad in a seed packet with two or three different greens in the mix. Over time we grew comfortable ordering our own combinations of greens and were never disappointed.

You can begin to harvest the plants when they are two to three inches tall and have well defined leaves. If you pull off leaves, be sure to harvest the plant before it bolts (forming seeds), as the leaves will become bitter. Harvest early the morning of delivery to ensure freshness. For a Famer's Market, we combined plants and/or leaves into quart-sized plastic bags. They sold out quickly and generated a great return.

Keep in mind that microgreens germinate in half the time of regular lettuce, so start your lettuce plants earlier. They all germinate in soil 50-65 degrees in temperature, so be sure to match a cooler fish with this crop.

Arugula is very popular and it adds a certain zing to salads. We settled on a 1:5 ratio. For every five regular lettuce varieties, we grew one arugula. The average shopper tasting arugula will turn up his/her nose, but tasting it inside a salad, will love the way it sharpens the overall flavor.

One part of our mix was always endive (city cousin of escarole). It is very attractive in a salad, because of its deep green color and ruffled leaves. This lettuce has just a little bite to it and complements the arugula without being overpowered by it.

A third microgreen in the mix was garden cress. It has a mild flavor and you can grow either the broadleaf or curly variety for a lovely addition to the salad plate.

One of the mix was always a romaine lettuce. It takes twice as much time to germinate as the microgreens, and it needs to have larger leaves to harvest, so plan your calendar accordingly. We like to pull off individual leaves rather than trying to harvest entire heads.

Our last in the mix is a ruby lettuce, for color and texture. You'll find a lot of varieties, and we love them all. In every garden salad we sold, it was the ruby lettuce that turned heads and opened the purses.

A smaller setup can also accommodate kale. Don't leave it out of your plans. Health enthusiasts clamor for it and even die hard skeptics will try it if you include a recipe, and be happy to come back for more.

Learn how to stagger your crops. Most of your greens can be planted every three weeks to ensure an ongoing harvest. How does this translate into profit? You can expect anywhere from $15 to $20 US dollars per square foot of aquaponic gardening. Remember that you can grow plants densely per square foot, since the roots don't spread through the soil and need all that space to absorb nutrients.

We didn't sell many harvested herbs, and for good reason. For one thing, once harvested, their shelf life is very limited. Second, not many people are accustomed to cooking with fresh herbs. For the sake of convenience and economy, most buy dried herbs at their local supermarkets and are content with that.

Aquaponic gardening is by far the most productive way to earn some cash from your garden. Enjoy it as a hobbyist and let it grow naturally into a commercial enterprise. As you are ready to transition, you'll need to draw up a business plan with a financial statement that includes your cash flow, the cost of broadening your enterprise and how you plan on marketing your produce. Many limit their enterprises to one or two crops and market those as specialty items. It eliminates the need for meeting so many different requirements of large and small vegetables, and some items offer higher returns than others. Do your research and decide exactly what you want to sell and how to sell it.

Be sure to apply for and obtain your certification for organically grown produce. This means organic seeds, and no pesticides, chemicals, or artificial fertilizers. This is easy when your garden is aquaponic.

Look into obtaining a business license and make sure you have a bank account for dedicated funds. Registering your business legally makes it easier to conduct it without problems later. No matter where you live, there will be statutes regulating the growing or selling of your produce. Knowing those laws and being in compliance saves hefty fees and heartache later on.

To make this a profitable venture, you need to keep track of your costs:

Output	Cost
Plants	
Plants	
Plants	
Plants	
Plants	
Vendor Fees	
Utility/Maintenance Costs	
Total Costs	
Sales	
Bottom Line (subtract sales from costs)	

Keep a record of your building costs, and extrapolate them over a two or three season period to determine ultimate profitability. You need to recoup your costs, but it doesn't have to be in one year. Your system will last a long time, and you'll be depreciating it in your taxes over ten years, so prorate your initial investment over that same period of time.

As with any business, network with your community. Join a local Chamber of Commerce. Talk to other gardeners. You never know where your next great lead will come from, so don't limit yourself. You can learn as much from your potential buyers as from other growers. Get to know your customers.

Don't forget that the scarcity of great greens in the winter months is like money in the bank for you. Having your system productive just as local farmers get blown away by frigid temperatures or snowstorms is a plus for you.

Last but not least, consider adopting a model like the Community Supported Agriculture (CSA) type of initiative. Local customers buy shares of your produce in the planting stage. In return, they get to take part in making decisions on what to grow and also earn a percentage of the harvest. You enjoy the profit of invested money and lower the risk of loss. They enjoy the fresh produce without doing any of the work in growing it. This is a win/win situation.

Be ready to explain the benefits of your business plan:

- Locally grown and sold produce reduces food miles. This is a term describing the distance food has traveled from harvest to market shelf. Locally grown produce uses less gasoline, reducing reliance on outside markets and on fossil fuels.

- It encourages local enterprise. Utilizing sustainable practices and obtaining organic certification, you demonstrate a model others can emulate.
- It promotes genetic integrity. Growing organic seeds, especially heirloom seeds, preserves the diversity of our produce.
- It keeps local money within the community.
- It lowers food costs for the community. Locally grown food incurs less overhead and can be marketed at a savings for local families.
- It forms alliances with other small businesses, particularly restaurants. In the process, all benefit from the increased connectivity.
- It brings families and communities together. Food is a great climate for conversation and for friendship.

Be realistic and know what the critics will say before you float your idea and look for financial backing. Depending on your resourcefulness and ingenuity, it can be costly to set up a system large enough to earn an adequate salary. Some large scale commercial enterprises range from $2000 to $10,000 for their startup investment. Someone somewhere will suggest this, and you need a solid explanation for why your system won't be nearly that expensive.

AQUAPONICS GARDENING

Aquaponics uses up a lot of power, so factor that cost into your business plan. Do you have any energy alternatives you can utilize? What will you do when the power goes out?

An aquaponic garden is not portable. What will you do if you need to move it at some point in time? That, and aquaponic gardening needs some daily maintenance. Are you a person who follows through on your commitments? An aquaponic garden requires you know your fish and your food intimately—do you? I'm not trying to be hard-nosed here, just realistic. Any banker who is being asked to front you $5,000 to start your business is going to ask these same questions.

When you have your business outline and you can answer any curve ball with an intelligent response, you're ready to expand your hobby to the big leagues.

AQUAPONICS GARDENING

Chapter Summary

An aquaponic garden is ideal for a commercial enterprise. You are able to grow a denser crop and harvest organic produce easily.

- The easiest crop for a hobby gardener is a lettuce bowl medley.
- Keep track of costs to see if this is a profitable venture for you.
- Develop a business plan if you want to expand this into a full time business.

In the next chapter, you will learn how to prepare some of the foods you may not be accustomed to right now. It's always good to salivate (oops, I meant dream) over the good food coming your way.

AQUAPONICS GARDENING

CHAPTER SIXTEEN

MAKE GREAT FOOD

No book on aquaponic gardening would be complete without enticing you with the promise of wonderful food and tempting recipes. Assuming you aren't growing orchids and roses, you may be interested in the practical aspect of feeding you and your family. There is something innately wholesome about freshly grown food, and my hope is to inspire you to try your hand.

Fresh food offers several benefits.

- First and foremost, fresh vegetables contain all of the vitamins and minerals they are meant to have as nature's food boosters. Vegetables retrieved from cans lose so much of their innate vitality in the preservation process and in the cooking process. Even eating healthy vegetables purchased from a local market results in declining nutritional values with each hour it sits in transit and at the market. For this reason, it's healthier to grow and pick your own as you prepare dinner.

- Foods picked ahead of their normal harvest dates to be delivered to local markets lose much of their flavor in preservation or in early harvest. In short, freshly grown food is simply delicious.
- Your produce will be preservative and pesticide free.
- Your food will build bridges and memories within the family and community. People remember sitting around a table, visiting and sharing recipes. Build the life you want to live.

Much of your garden produce can be saved for winter consumption. Root vegetables can be stored in a cool, dry place and complemented with fresh herbs. This lowers your grocery bills and provides a nice variety to the fresh vegetables you're growing in your aquaponic garden.

You can extend your meals with bits and pieces of what you grow. Add extra vegetables to bulk your menu, while boosting its nutritional value. Leftover scraps of tomatoes and peppers are great in omelettes. Bits of veggies taste great in soups or stews. I cook extra tomatoes down into sauce and freeze it if I'm not making spaghetti or some other Italian dish right away.

A tremendous savings takes place when you grow and use your own produce. Here are some recipes I'd love to share with you. They represent many a meal around our table, and hope you enjoy them as well.

Simple Salad with Vinaigrette

Lettuce greens
2 slices bacon, cut into small pieces

Vinaigrette

1 Tbsp Dijon Mustard
Splash of dry white wine
¼ cup of vinegar (balsamic, walnut, etc.)
¼ cup vegetable oil
½ cup extra virgin olive oil
1 Tbsp cream

1. Prepare your salad bowl of mixed greens, tearing large pieces into bite-sized morsels.
2. Sautee' bacon in a hot pan with a splash of olive oil.
3. Liquefy your mustard with a splash of dry white wine in a small mixing bowl.
4. Whisk the vegetable oil into your mustard.
5. Whisk in the olive oil when the mustard has been emulsified. (Olive oil gets bitter when whipped.)
6. Add cream at the end.

Combine your greens with the bacon pieces, pour vinaigrette on top, and toss.

Herbed Vinegars

- Use any flavor of vinegar you prefer. A nice apple cider, red wine, or balsamic vinegar are my favorites. Apple cider vinegars marry themselves well with fruit infusions, while a nice balsamic or red wine vinegar complements stronger flavors.

- Use two to three sprigs of fresh herbs

1. Place two cups of vinegar into a sterile quart canning jar.
2. Add 2-3 sprigs of fresh herbs. I love a combination of basil, rosemary and thyme.
3. Place a square of waxed paper over the top and seal with a ring.
4. Shake and let it develop rich flavor for a month. Shake every now and then. The vinegar will corrode a jar seal, so be sure to keep your waxed paper in place.

Pesto

2 cups basil
2 cloves garlic
¼ cup pine nuts
⅔ cups extra virgin olive oil
salt and pepper

Place all ingredients into a blender and run until smooth.

Use the pesto to garnish cooked pasta or fish.

Salsa

Chopped tomatoes
1 peeled and chopped mango
1 peeled and cubed avocado
½ cup minced fresh cilantro
½ cup rinsed black beans
½ cup chopped red onion

AQUAPONICS GARDENING

3 or 4 peeled and chopped jalapeno peppers (wear gloves)
3 Tbsp freshly squeezed lime juice
1 Tbsp extra virgin olive oil
2 cloves minced garlic
½ tsp salt.

Mix all ingredients in a bowl. I eyeball the tomatoes and taste it until I have the right ratio. Let it chill before using it as a garnish or serving with chips.

Sauteed Vegetable Plate

Equal portions sliced carrots, whole green beans, colorful peppers, onion
Splash extra virgin olive oil
Splash dry white wine
Splash balsamic vinegar
Handful dried cranberries
Handful sliced almonds
1 Tbsp butter

1. Heat a large skillet and then melt the butter. Add the almonds and lightly toast them. Remove the walnuts and return the skillet to the stove.
2. Heat your skillet once again and add your olive oil.
3. When the oil starts to flow like water, add your sliced vegetables.
4. Sear your vegetables, then toss and let them get crispy around the edges.
5. Add the white wine; scrape up the pan's little pieces.
6. Add the craisins, and let warm until they are soft.

7. Add the almonds. Stir slightly, and pour the mixture into a serving bowl.

Flamed-Kissed Grilled Veggies

Our family loves an outdoor gathering in the spring, summer, and fall. We often throw a bowl of tossed veggies on the side of the grill, and if we want to be formal, thread them onto skewers. Remember that wooden skewers need to be soaked in water to prevent them from catching on fire. I've made that mistake once before! Most usually I toss them into a grill basket and set them directly on the grill.

Here's my bouquet of grilled produce.

Garlic: 30 minutes for a whole head. Set the garlic bulb on foil and drizzle with extra virgin olive oil and a sprinkle of salt.. Wrap it in foil and pinch the top closed.

Onions: 25 minutes. Peel and cut into quarters.

Peppers: 20 minutes. Cut into halves or quarters and remove the seeds.

Potatoes: 15 minutes. Slice into ¼ inch pieces. Parboil for a couple minutes. Drain and coat them with extra virgin olive oil, sprinkle salt and pepper.

Green beans: 10 minutes. Snap off the ends.

Squash: 10 minutes. Cut into large chunks.

Lettuce: 5 to 10 minutes. A head of Romaine works well. Char it lightly, but don't cook it all the way through.

Tomatoes: 5 minutes. Cut into chunks or quarters.

Your veggies will be fork tender when they are done.

Garden Fresh Minestrone Soup

Parboil a dried bean bouquet. I like a combination of navy beans and pinto beans. Simmer them in four quarts of vegetable or chicken stock for an hour or two. Drain your beans in a colander and rinse them. (I know you'll lose your B vitamins by rinsing them, but you'll also lose the gas, and your family will thank you.) Add your freshly shelled beans and cook for another hour or so, until all of the beans are tender. I usually figure about four to five cups of cooked beans are a good base. Set them aside in a bowl.

Soup ingredients:

3 Tbsp butter
4 large, chopped onions
10 garlic cloves, finely minced
1 mildly hot or flavorful pepper, finely diced
2 chopped sweet peppers
6 to 8 large tomatoes, chopped, with juices

½ cup dry white wine
1 cup diced carrots
2 cups corn kernels
3 cups cooked pasta of choice
3 cups kale

Seasoning bouquet:

2 tsp savory
1 tsp oregano
½ tsp rosemary
½ tsp thyme
salt and pepper to taste

1. Melt the butter in a large skillet and saute the onion and garlic. Add peppers and cook until all veggies are soft.
2. Add the white wine, stirring up all the crispy little pieces of veggies.
3. Add tomatoes and increase the heat, stirring, reducing the mixture for about five minutes.
4. Move your sauteed mix into the bean pot. Add all your seasonings.
5. Add the rest of your veggies, and cooked pasta. Let them simmer for about 20 minutes, mixing all those luscious flavors.
6. Chop your kale and add in the last five minutes before serving.
7. Garnish with minced flat leaf parsley and basil.

Fish Under Cover

Fish
3 lb fish fillets
2 Tbsp butter
1 onion, peeled and chopped
1 clove minced garlic
1 Tbsp chicken bouillon or fish paste
1 tsp black pepper
¼ cup dry white wine

Filling
2 sticks butter
1 ¼ cup flour
3 cups hot chicken broth
1 cup warmed cream
small handful crushed thyme leaves
2 large carrots cut into coins and cooked until tender
1 cup peas

Crust
2 cups sifted flour
1 tsp salt
⅔ cup cold butter
4-5 Tbsp cold water

For the fish: Melt your butter in a skillet until it bubbles. Add the onion and garlic, cook until transparent. Add the crushed bouillon or fish paste, stirring. Lay the cod on your bed of vegetables and add the white wine. Let simmer on low as the fish cooks.

For the filling: In a medium saucepan, melt the butter over medium heat until it is foamy. Add the flour a bit at a time, creating a roux. Let it brown slightly. Stir in chicken broth a little at a time, constantly whisking. Add the thyme leaves as it bubbles and thickens. Add the cooked carrots and peas.

For the crust: Put the flour and salt into a mixing bowl, and stir to mix. Cut in the cold butter. Add the water, stir, then turn out on pastry sheet. Roll out the bottom crust and lay it in a pie plate. Add the fish and then pour the creamy filling. Roll out and lay the second crust on top of the pie. Create vent holes for steam and crimp edges.

Bake the fish pie at 425 degrees for 35-40 minutes.

Rib-Sticking Pasta Salad

Salad Bed

2 medium zucchini, sliced
2 cups peas
1 head broccoli, cut into florets
¼ cut green onions, sliced
2 cloves minced garlic
1 lb cooked bowtie pasta

Dressing
¼ herbed vinegar

¼ cup honey
¼ cup freshly squeezed lemon juice
2 Tbsp chopped chives
2 Tbsp minced flat leaf Italian parsley
3 Tbsp dijon mustard
Splash dry white wine
salt and pepper to taste

Topper:
2 cups cooked fish, poached in white wine and seasoned with a handful of thyme.

Prepare the **Dressing**
1. Liquefy your mustard with a splash of dry white wine in a small mixing bowl.
2. Whisk the vinegar and honey into the mustard mixture.
3. Add the herbs and spices.

Toss the vegetables with the cooked, cooled pasta.
Add the dressing and toss to coat well.
Lay the fish on top of the bed of pasta.

Fish Cakes

6 Tbsp butter, divided
1 small onion, minced
2 cloves minced garlic
1 pound fresh fish, chopped
¼ cup mayonnaise
1 large egg, slightly beaten
1 Tbsp Dijon mustard
1 Tbsp soy sauce

1 Tbsp lemon juice
¼ tsp hot sauce
Salt and pepper
3 cups breadcrumbs, divided into one cup and two cups

1. Melt 2 Tbsp butter in a large skillet.
2. Add the onion and garlic, cook until tender, remove from heat.
3. Place the sauteed vegetables in a bowl with the fish pieces.
4. Add the whisked egg and mayonnaise, stirring.
5. Add all the seasonings, stirring.
6. Add 2 cups of bread crumbs, stirring.
7. Fashion the mixture into eight fish cakes.
8. Coat each cake with the last of the bread crumbs.
9. Melt the remaining butter in the skillet. Let it sizzle and get foamy.
10. Lay the cakes into the butter and cook over medium-high heat 4 to 5 minutes on each side, until golden and fish is cooked.
11. Remove from skillet and pat with paper towels.

Sweet Corn Relish:

4 cups corn
2 large chopped tomatoes
3 green onions, sliced
¼ tsp herbed vinegar

Toss the vegetables together with the vinegar and garnish the fish cakes.

Chilli Rellenos with White Fish

AQUAPONICS GARDENING

1 lb cooked fish pieces
2 Tbsp butter
½ cup chopped onion
1-2 cups chopped green chilis
2 tsp marjoram
1 tsp cumin
1 ½ cup cream
¼ cup flour
4 beaten eggs
2 cups shredded cheese.

1. Melt the butter, adding the onion and chilies. Cook until tender.
2. Coat a baking dish with butter.
3. Mix the flour and cream until smooth. Add the eggs and beat well. Stir in spices.
4. Fold the cooked fish into the creamy mixture.
5. Pour the creamy mixture into prepared baking dish.
6. Top with cheese.
7. Bake at 350 degrees for 45-50 minutes, until a knife comes out clean.
8. Let it stand five minutes before serving.

Seafood Crepes

Filling:
2 Tbsp butter
2 Tbsp flour
¼ to ½ cup dry white wine
Chopped sage or basil or marjoram
Chunks of white fish.

1. Melt the butter and stir in the flour.
2. Let the roux brown before adding wine. Whisk.

3. Add the spices and the fish, and cover with a tight fitting lid. Let the seafood cook. When it is cooked through, remove it from the heat.

Crepe:

1 cup flour
1 ⅓ cup liquid, comprised of milk and water
¼ tsp salt
3 Tbsp butter

1. Mix the flour, liquid and seasoning in a blender and refrigerate.
2. Melt the butter in the skillet until it dances.
3. Pour ½ cup of mixture into the pan and tip the pan so it fills the bottom.
4. Let it brown, flip it, and when the second side is brown, lift it out.
5. Lay it on a plate with a layer of waxed paper between each crepe.

When the crepes are cooked, lay one on each plate. Add filling and roll it. Garnish with a sprig of rosemary.

AQUAPONICS GARDENING

PART IV

THE SCIENCE BEHIND AQUAPONIC GARDENING

CHAPTER SEVENTEEN

GLOSSARY OF TERMS

aerating pump — All of God's creatures need oxygen, and fish are no exception. A little explanation of how your fish will use it illustrates the importance of supplying this basic life sustaining element. Fish may not have lungs, but they still need air to breathe, filtering dissolved oxygen from the water through their gills.

The gills (usually four on each side) are situated just behind the head, and are a series of bony flaps with filaments. Just as the human bronchus divides again and again to form a pulmonary tree for oxygen intake and exchange, the gill filaments support a network of lamellae. Water runs through the gills and those busy little filaments employ osmotic action to extract oxygen from the water with carbon dioxide being released in the exchange. That precious life sustaining oxygen is directly absorbed into the fish's bloodstream.

Atmospheric oxygen comprises about 20% of the air we breathe, but that number is significantly reduced when we talk about dissolved oxygen in a fish tank. The amount of dissolved oxygen in the water decreases as the water temperature rises. Take a look at Chapter Ten, in which the water temperatures for various fishes are listed. At 59 degrees Fahrenheit the water will absorb less than 5% of the oxygen available from the air, 4.35% to be exact. That figure decreases for every degree of temperature as the water warms. Hence the need for an aeration pump.

How do you choose one? I'm glad you asked. Here are some of my top picks:

The Tetra Easy Whisper Air Pump is an excellent choice. Its manufacturer claims its quiet sound is a result of its domed surface reducing the noise of the engine. If your tank is clear and you want to enjoy your fish as they swim around, this one will provide bubbles to increase your viewing pleasure. It comes with a lifetime guarantee, which is a plus if you're not wanting to fix a breakdown yourself.

It comes in five graduated sizes for whatever scale you have designed for your fish tank. The company reviews are not the best, but check out the website for yourself.

The Hygger 16mm air pump is another great option. It is quiet, and appropriate for a tank up to six feet deep, pumping 16 L/min of air. It comes with just a one year warranty, is not recommended for use out of doors, and should not get wet.

The Active Aqua air pump is seven inches in diameter and not submersible. It offers a lot of aeration and is fairly quiet, and comes with a detailed set of instructions for installation. The system is energy efficient, but don't use it if your aquaponic garden is out of doors.

For a smaller tank (50-160 gallons), the Fluval q2 pump is a good alternative. It is low maintenance and inexpensive to set up, although you will need an aerator for the tank. It is designed with a dual wall chamber to muffle noise, has replaceable diaphragms, and circulates 25 L/min in air flow.

A fifth great option is the Mylivell pump. It is not waterproof and attaches via a suction cup to the outside of your tank. It is low voltage and runs with no motor, making it one of the quietest options available. This is suitable for a smaller set up.

Be aware that many of these don't come with tubing, so read the fine print to be sure you have everything you need when it's time to install it.

algae — Those nasty green strands in your tank are quite a nuisance, but worse, they can destroy your aquaponic garden. Algae are organisms growing in your water. Some are just single-celled organisms, and others grow in colonies creating chloroplasts as they grow. Left unchecked, they can cloud your water and make it feel foul. Worse, algae affects your pH level and uses precious oxygen in their growth.

Let's look at the oxygen issues first. Your fish need oxygen, and the last thing you want is to find them asphyxiated one morning due to oxygen depletion through the night. How does that happen, and what does algae have to do with it? Like all plants, algae will produce oxygen during daily photosynthesis. At night, when there is no light for photosynthesis, these strands will start to use your tank's reservoir of dissolved oxygen for their own growth, resulting in lower levels for your fish. If your fish appear to be suffering despite high oxygen levels, check your readings during the middle of the night. You may find them extremely low. Worse yet, when algae begins to die, the cells consume oxygen to decompose and further deplete your oxygen reservoir.

Algae also affects your delicate pH balance. These, as in photosynthesis, relate to the rising and the setting of the sun, and are called diurnal swings. As algae consume CO_2 during the day, they raise the water pH, making it more basic. The readings fluctuate based on when photosynthesis ends, and your water pH will lower, becoming more acidic. Keeping your system in balance becomes tricky and time-consuming.

AQUAPONICS GARDENING

The best solution lies in preventing it. Make sure you maintain proper pH and oxygen levels in your water and make sure your pump keeps water moving without stagnation. Look at your water's phosphorus level. If you see it begin, try to control the amount of growth. Shading your water will decrease its formation, since algae needs sunlight to grow.

Filtration also helps. If you have the ingenuity and time to put together the filters, screens, and devices to remove uneaten food, waste and decaying plants, you can prevent the buildup of algae. Depending on what kind of filter you use, you'll cycle your water through pads, sponges, or wool to snag the waste before it is returned to the tank. You'll need to periodically clean your filter. Take it from the tank, clean it in clear water, and quickly return it, turning everything on again. One caveat: Use something other than tap water so you don't kill your cultured bacteria.

In addition to mechanical filtration, systems employing chemicals are also available. Buying a system can be expensive, but you have to counter that against the cost of losing your crop or seeing your fish die. Which scenario do you want to manage? I have found the purchase of a filtration system more valuable than trial and error, and favor mechanical systems over biological or chemical strategies.

An aquarium filter pad in one easy option. It is adaptable to any size or shape required, and inexpensive. You'll need to replace it every three to four weeks, so establish a regimen and way to keep track of time.

Another method utilizes activated charcoal, which comes in pellets. You can grind it to the size of product you want, using either the pellets or reducing it to a fine powder. It works quickly and efficiently, and is less unsightly.

A third option is a reusable medium that functions in a different way. These are shaped like tiny little hexagrams to increase the surface area of water to filtration media, and function very efficiently.

Look at all of the products available and read reviews to select the one you wish to use. The point is to be proactive and reduce algae immediately. Cleaning your tank keeps your fish healthy and your water levels within normal limits.

biofilter — You'll hear this term a lot in aquaponic gardening, but it isn't complicated. A biofilter serves to extend your bed of microbes, converting fish waste to plant food. Yes, it's really that simple. It becomes an important consideration when you are submerging your plants into the water rather than cultivating them in a growth medium like hydroton pellets.

AQUAPONICS GARDENING

If you have a large operation with a raft of bedding plants and surface water to spare, you can utilize a floating medium like K1 media to increase the surface area of microbes and provide adequate fertilization. You can also install static trays or drip filters and cycle your water through them between the solid waste filter and the submerged plants.

Your need for a biofilter is determined by the density of your fish population relative to the volume of water, as well as how many plants you want to grow. If you maintain a small number of fish and don't overfeed them, you are going to be producing less solid waste and may be able to get by without a biofilter.

deep water culture — This growing technique involves a deeper water supply with floating plants that rest on the surface, their roots submerged in the water. It alleviates the need for canals or tubes, pumping the water through a series of tanks, and is scalable from the tiniest of ambitions to large rafts of plants grown for commercial purposes.

ebb and flow — This system of watering and feeding your plants is centuries old, and remains one of the simplest forms of aquaponic today. It is also known as a flood and drainage system. You will create your "flood table" by growing produce in a plastic tray with your growth medium positioned above the tank reservoir. Several times each day your sump pump is turned on to pump your watery stew up a pipe, emptying into your grow tray. Let it sit there and drain slowly until the next scheduled flooding/feeding for your plants. You can install a timer to handle the process automatically.

fish food — What food and how much of it are you going to be getting? Nelson Pade offers a great organic, non-GMO food for fish, available in small or large bags online. You can also buy fish food from local pet stores or a nearby WalMart. What you feed fish is determined by the type of fish you're growing, but realize a few basic things. First, when you buy any kind of fish food, it will be loaded with a good mix of nutrients, a balance of protein, carbs, fats, and minerals. That's why it's so expensive.

Others opt for making their own. If you're wanting to reduce costs, try duckweed, digging worms from the backyard, or slipping some larvae into your tank. If your fish are picky and won't eat these delicacies, you'll have to gather the remains to avoid excess strain on your filters.

genetically modified organisms — Agribusinesses began experimenting with ways to improve on Mother Nature and devised ways of modifying the genetic structure of the food we eat. Their good intentions of reducing food shortages unleashed a storm of controversy over the benefits versus the harms of ingesting GMOs.

AQUAPONICS GARDENING

The rise in food-based allergies has risen from 3.4% in the late nineties to more than 5% in 2011. There is no evidence that genetically modified foods are responsible, but there is no evidence that it's not, either. The rising incidence of cancer worldwide, along with the increased development of superbugs, all provide fodder for the arguments against genetically modified foods. Again, there is no proof either way, but might I just suggest that it's not natural?

grow lights — Who has enough sunlight for an indoor aquaponic garden? Not many of us. Luckily, you have choices, and you have three main considerations. First, look at its size to be sure it will meet your garden's needs. Second, look at how it attaches. Some screw into existing light sockets and others are mounted to the ceiling. Third, look at the light's features. What color light does it put out? Does it require regulating? Is it noisy? Most importantly, what kind of heat does it put out? I know. It sounds like way too much complication for something as simple as light, but nothing is simple when it comes to aquaponic gardening. This is science, people

The Feit hanging light is adaptable to either a flush or suspended attachment, and you can get various sizes ranging from 5 inches to 2 feet in diameter. It runs on 120 V electrical power and comes with a 2-year warranty. Be aware that it has a 5 foot cord, so take that into consideration.

This bamboo suspended light is affordable and offers the convenience of being scalable. You can stack them for expanding applications. The LED lights are economical and do not require adjustment as your plants grow. They are great for a small setup.

If you need a larger system, look at the Philizon system of lighting, made in China. These range from a smaller version available on Amazon as a 600 LCD variety, up to multiple bars for extensive growing.

herbs — These are great for aquaponic gardens, because unlike vegetables, you are growing small amounts to flavor dishes rather than whole meals.

Culinary herbs grow in a lot of different ways. Some are perennials, some look like small shrubs, and others like small trees. Thyme, sage, lavender, parsley, basil, rosemary, and bay are the most commonly grown herbs. There are over four hundred medicinal herbs you can grow, but it requires knowing how to use the herb. Some are steeped into teas. Some can be applied topically. Others may be ingested, but it isn't an exact science.

I'm a lover of the idea of homeopathic healing, but never courageous enough to grow my own and self-medicate. My recommendation: grow what you'll use to season your food.

high tunnel — This is a structure built and covered with plastic. It serves as a mini greenhouse and can be either a simple protective covering or a fancy one with installed watering systems, fans, and a heat source. Homesteaders have been jumping on the high tunnel bandwagon, and with good reason. Also known as hoophouses, these unheated structures extend the growing season. Both hobby gardeners and commercial growers have embraced them, especially since the USDA started their high tunnel initiative. They come in many different sizes and configurations, ranging from 1000 square feet to hooking several together, spanning multiple acres.

homeostasis— Simply defined, it is the process of supporting life by maintaining a balance of neutrality within the body or organism. If you can understand the process in your own body, you have a frame of reference for understanding what is happening in your aquaponic garden. Your body employs many compensatory mechanisms for maintaining the ideal blood sugar, blood pressure, body temperature, cellular water level, and pH, to name a few.

Your ideal body pH is 7.35 to 7.45. Within this narrow range, you are running your engines on all four cylinders. Suppose you start to hyperventilate. Your body will blow off carbon dioxide (CO_2), which is an acid, in each breath. That loss of CO_2 will make your blood more alkaline, lowering your blood pH. To compensate, your kidneys will kick in, excreting bicarb

(HCO_3), which is alkaline, and voila, your blood pH returns to a level within its normal range.

hydroponics — Literally, this means growing plants in water. Because many of the same principles are employed in an aquaponic garden, remember, one part of the word is derived from *hydroponic*, let's look at your options. Get a firm understanding of these principles before designing your system.

Six types of hydroponic gardens may be constructed, and the first three require more ingenuity, or trial and error, than the latter three.

- The wick system is used by inserting a wick (think of a candle wick) into the plant container, which draws the water up to feed and water the roots.
- A water culture system employs lightweight containers holding plants that float in the water, directly absorbing the chemically laden water.
- An ebb and flow system requires immersing one plant in water and then draining it into from one to the other, and so on. It requires a pumping mechanism to regulate the flow of water.
- A drip system requires a pump with a timer, which as you would guess, drips water onto the plants at appropriate intervals.

- A nutrient film is used in both hydroponic and aquaponic gardening, pumping the chemically fertilized water constantly through the roots.

hydroton — These little gems are a form of dried clay broken up and baked into small pellets. If you've ever rooted plants in a glass of water, you know that the plant languishes against the side of the glass because its stem has no support of its own. Your plants need some sort of structure for growing straight and tall. The most often source in aquaponic gardening is hydroton pellets.

Most gardening centers offer bags of vermiculite and other soil-based media in large displays. Before entering the world of aquaponic gardening, I wasn't familiar with it either, but I soon learned it offered five benefits:

1. The little pellets are filled with tiny pores, and they are like sponges growing on the ocean floor. They absorb water, but drain out excess if you use them in a soil-based application. For our purposes, they hold water and provide surface area for necessary bacterial growth.
2. These clay baked pellets hold their shape over time, not needing to be replaced as often, and allowing your plant roots to continuously exchange nitrogen to oxygen.
3. The pellets maintain the proper acid/base balance in your garden.

4. The pellets are produced in gigantic kilns and the high temperature results in a sterile product. You want to grow your own bacteria, not introduce microbes toxic for either plants or fish into the mix.
5. Hydroton pellets are reusable. You can rinse them out and use them over and over again. What a bargain!

LECA aggregates — There are a number of grow media out there. All of the pebbles in this category will work for you. You'll need small net pots 1.5 to 2.5 inches in diameter. Soak your pebbles and place seeds on top, covering them with one or two water-soaked pebbles, depending on recommended planting depth. Hydroton is a brand of pellets, usually manufactured by heating clay in a rotating kiln. As it heats, the clay expands and forms pellets with incredibly increased surface areas for cultivating the bacteria you need as a growth medium.

When you open the package, soak them for 4 to 6 hours to remove dust, as well as to be sure they won't float in your system. Some forms will not be good for the pH of your water. How do you tell? Do a vinegar test. Put a small handful of pellets in a glass of vinegar. If bubbles rise to the surface, it has too much limestone in its composition and won't work for your system. Always look for smaller pellets, because the larger ones have more air space. You're wanting the highest porous surface area possible.

media bed — This system will look more like traditional gardening, since larger pots or trays hold the LECA (Lightweight Expanded Clay Aggregate) pellets, and the plant grows looking like its traditional counterpart. The bed needs to be about 12 inches deep, and it increases the cost substantially.

The container you choose may be the most important decision you'll make. It will take up the largest amount of space, and it will need a depth best suited for the plants you want to grow. Fill it with pebbles, usually Hydroton, to within two inches of the top. Remember that 12 inches is recommended. This grow bed acts as the biofilter.

If you are building a tower system with PVC pipes as your gardening bed, you're going to be investing in a lot more pellets. Don't skimp here. Less is not more, more is more.

nitrogen cycle — This is the process sustaining life on planet earth. While nitrogen in its gaseous state comprises about 87% of our atmosphere, its life-sustaining qualities are not accessible by our bodies in its gaseous state.

1. Scientists call the first step in the cycle nitrogen fixation. Bacteria convert fish waste into ammonia. Ammonia (if you remember back to chemistry class) is chemically known NH_3, and the process of nitrification begins.

2. In nitrification, bacteria transform NH_3 to NO_3, which plants utilize as a nitrate fertilizer.

In aquaponic gardening, the most important part of this cycle of life isn't either the fish or the plants. It's the growth medium. The Nitrogen Cycle takes place on the growth medium, most often hydroton pellets, where the nitrifying bacteria find a home and carry out this important part of the process.

nutrient film — A nutrient film is a thin layer of nutrient-rich water that flows through plant roots for absorption. In hydroponic watering systems (which aquaponics is, merely replacing fish with chemicals), the water is distributed in channels, often without the aid of pumps. The slope of the channel, the rate at which the water flows, and the right size of the channelling system, work together to create this perfect system for healthy plant growth. You'll read about wicking and ebb and flow in hydroponic gardening, but don't get overwhelmed. We eliminate the mystique in aquaponic gardening by using a small pump, which eliminates the need for a degree in physics, resulting in water being distributed automatically.

organic gardening — Organic gardening is pure and unadulterated growth of plants without chemical fertilizers, herbicides, or pesticides. Many claim that these have been linked to breast cancer, damaged brain function, Parkinson's disease, miscarriages, birth defects, autism, prostate cancer, non-Hodgkin's lymphoma, and infertility. Please realize a link is not definitive proof of causation, but it's enough to make a thinking person go, "Hmmm." There are other benefits as well. Many believe the compounded toxicity of constantly pouring chemicals into our soil, worldwide, will be catastrophic in years to come. Aquaponics offers a 100% organic gardening experience.

pH balance — Maintaining a neutral acid/base balance in your water is a matter of regulating the chemical reactions taking place. This is achieved, in part, by the nitrogen cycle, and nitrification forms the chemical basis for sustaining the aquatic and plant life in your aquaponic garden. Here's how the cycle is played out in your little microcosm of underwater drama. Your fish eat and convert their ingested proteins into ammonia (NH_3) and ammonium (NH_4+).

The ammonia in their water is toxic for the fish, so it is imperative that the process of nitrification begins to take place immediately. The normal and beneficial bacteria in your water will colonize in the media you've installed in your tank (usually clay pebbles like hydroton). One of those beneficial bacteria is nitrosomonas, and it chemically transforms the ammonia into ammonium by combining with the oxygen you are pumping into your water through the aerator. Here's what takes place:

$NH_3 + O_2 \rightarrow NO_2 + 3H^+ + 2e^-$

This represents the first step in nitrification. The second step is the introduction of a second equally important bacteria, nitrobacter, which completes the process of turning ammonia into nitrate, i.e., plant food. Here's what takes place:

$NO_2 + H_2O \rightarrow NO_3 + 2H^+ + 2e^-$

Those two loose electrons are absorbed into the water, making it more acidic and thereby increasing the pH. Your test kit will measure levels of nitrate, nitrite, and ammonia within your water, so you can track the process from day to day.

photosynthesis— You heard all about this in school, but it probably went in one ear and out the other. Now, it's time to get serious and be sure you understand what's involved. You know it's a chemical process in which plants take sunlight and convert its energy into chloroplasts, keeping plants green and healthy. In this give and take reaction, water transfers electrons to carbon dioxide to produce carbohydrates. During the reaction the carbon dioxide loses electrons and the water become oxidized. The cycle is Mother Nature's way of keeping all of the plants and animals happy through mutually beneficial trades.

sump pump— Don't skimp on your pump. As you're counting the cost in building your aquaponic garden, there's always the temptation to channel your money into a fancier aquarium or into more fish. Resist that temptation. Your ecosystem will only be as good as its bones, and you need to invest in the right equipment. Here are my top five picks:

Coming in three sizes, the Fluval Hagen Sea Pumps are as good as any on the market. Its patented Smart-Pump™ technology, offered in both the SP4/SP6 models, actually monitors its efficiency and shuts off in the event of overheating. Its cool operation will not affect water temperature, a huge plus. Because it isn't metal, nothing will corrode in outdoor humidity or exposure to water in the tank. It is submersible, but can also run outside of the tank. Be aware that it's not the quietest out there, but if your system is in the basement or out of doors, that may not be a problem.

A second option to consider is the Aqueon. Noted for an adjustable flow rate, it offers you a lot more control over your new ecosystem. The manufacturers claim it is quiet, but reviewers are not 100% on this feature. It is easy to install and it is submersible, so it's suitable for an outdoor garden.

The Jebao DCP Sine Wave Submersible Pump is perfect for a larger aquaponic garden. It is submersible, powerful, and relatively quiet. It will not affect water temperature inside of your tank. It is one of five Jebao models to choose from, so do your homework and look at all of the options before making a purchase.

I am also impressed with the Eheim models. This company makes pumps for ponds as well as several options for varying sizes of aquariums. The Universal 600 comes in both a larger and more compact model. It comes with a removable prefilter and is designed for quiet efficiency. The downside? As you might expect, it's not the cheapest pump on the market. My sainted mother always said, "You only get what you pay for," and in this instance, she is right. I think it's worth the money.

My fifth fave is the Uniclife model. The DEP-400 is equipped with a memory function to store settings, handy when you want to shut it down or lower its output, making it easier to set back up again. It is manufactured with an intake screen which serves as a mini-filter to help keep out debris. The manufacturers suggest it to be run under water to keep the engine cool, but you know what that means, don't you? It will raise water temperature. On the plus side, it is energy efficient.

Do your homework. Look at the manufacturing specs, talk to people in the know. Check out pet stores, as well as professionals at Grainger. If you're building a tower of growing beds, you'll need more of a professional grade pump, so plan accordingly.

sustainability — We live in a delicate relationship with our home on Earth, and everything we do affects that relationship. When we grow and consume responsibly, nature and man live hand in hand. Our goal is to live *with* our environment. Nurture it, not plunder it. For too many years we have looked at the earth as a magical genie, stripping its natural resources with no thought of the consequences. Sustainability is a new way of looking at our earth home, and using our resources in a way that ensures future generations never get left with a bankrupt environment.

In 1969, the United States adopted The National Environmental Policy Act "to create and maintain conditions under which humans and nature can exist in productive harmony, that permit fulfilling the social, economic, and other requirements of present and future generations." To this end, the EPA established strategies that keep man and nature in balance. Two of their most ambitious and worthwhile projects have been facilitating the rising number of high tunnels and solar panels installed across the country. Rebates and information have led many a seeker to a more sustainable lifestyle. Preppers and hobbyists both benefit from their initiatives.

symbiosis — In its most basic definition, symbiosis is the process of two organisms living together. In commensalism, one organism benefits from the other (think spider webs on trees). In parasitism, one lives off of the other (think tapeworms). In mutualism, both organisms benefit, as in aquaponics. Your bacteria are tiny one-celled organisms you want to nurture and give a home to, because they are exchanging the ammonia your fish excrete into valuable fertilizer for your plants. These beneficial bacteria are not causing disease or going to infect you, so no worries. This is a win/win situation for the fish and for the plants. Find symbiotic worksheets to learn more!

water testing kits — By now you realize the importance of monitoring your water. The most deluxe system will measure pH, oxygen, ammonia levels, nitrates, nitrites, general hardness and carbonate water hardness, potassium, iron, and trace elements. Let's look first at normal values.

- Your water pH needs to be between 6 and 8, with 6.5 being ideal.
- Ammonia measures read between 0.25 and 8.0 ppm of ammonia.
- A good kit will measure nitrites between 0.25 and 5.0 ppm of nitrites.
- Look for a kit that measures ranges of 5 - 160 ppm of nitrates.
- An idea kit will also measure general water hardness as well as mineral solution. The same elements that make your water hard or

soft will also affect your aquarium. If you use rain water, it should not contain minerals.

- Low potassium levels in the water will affect your plants. You can doctor that with additions of potassium hydroxide, which will raise your pH without making your water hard.
- Just like you, your plants need iron to grow lush green leaves.

Bear in mind that you aren't looking for a simple jar with test strips. You're not just measuring pH like you would for a swimming pool. This is science. Be thorough. Here are some of my top picks: Nelson Padeputs out a top of the line kit. They offer detailed instructions on using the kit and have a table with normal ranges.. Did I mention it was top of the line? Watch your jaw drop when you look it up, but it is very thorough.

Another option is from the LaMott company, with more than one kit advertised. This is another high end model, but with choices to make it more affordable.

At the other end of the spectrum is the Ultimate 14 in 1 jar with test strips, available on Amazon. As you would guess, it measures fourteen different levels and requires color coded assessment. Potassium and oxygen are not in that list.

The bottom line is simple: Test your water or risk losing both your fish and your plants. You don't need the most expensive system on the planet, but investing in quality makes a difference. My sainted mother always said, "You only get what you pay for," and in the world of aquaponic garden water testing, this is certainly true.

wicking system — This is a very simple way to transport your nutrient-laden water to your plant roots. Think of the way a paper towel utilizes capillary motion to draw moisture from a kitchen countertop. If you operate a small aquaponic garden, you can implement this age old strategy.

Wicking is a passive system whereby you draw water from your tank into your growing bed. You won't need expensive pumps, and instead install wicks comprised of rope or felt which will pull water upward. Be sure to keep your water level high enough that it doesn't have to be drawn very far.

This can be adapted for a crossover system utilizing both traditional growing media and nutrient-rich aquaponic water. Prepare a bed, and install a pipe for delivering water into the base of the bed. The water travels upward to meet the plant roots without the need to water from above.

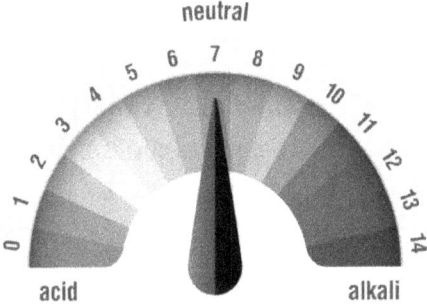

FINAL WORDS

By now you're an expert on aquaponic gardening. You've learned about what it is and isn't and you're sold on its benefits. Take a moment and list the reasons why you want to start one. See how your list compares to mine:

- Year round fresh produce
- Organic and non-GMO produce at a price I can afford
- A small side gig growing plants for others

These are all valuable reasons for diving into the world of aquaponics. If you're a prepper or survivalist, this is right up your alley. If you're a gardener, this is the best thing since sliced bread. And if you are wanting to put fresh food on the table, this book has been written for you.

We discussed in detail the concept behind aquaponic gardening. You know by now that the nitrogen cycle is your friend. Read and reread the explanations of how to grow a nutritious watery stew for plants and fish. Find a friend and explain it. If you're like me, you can read it and say, "Uh, huh. I get it." A week later it's like a vacuum in my brain sucked it all away. It's not until I read it, digest the information, and then explain it to someone else that it earns a place inside of my head. Your understanding of the concepts is the key to your success.

Be sure you understand all the readings required in using a test kit. Put together a system for tracking measurements with dates and norms in the very first column. If you have it ready, you'll use it. I know from personal experience that it's all too easy to test the water, and think. "Hmph. That's interesting. I wonder what it will be tomorrow." The next day I test the water and think, "Hmph. That's interesting." By the third day, I no longer remember the first day's readings and only a vague idea of where I've been or where I'm wanting to be. Keeping a record of your results is how you most quickly produce the optimal watery blend for your plants and it is the basis for each adjustment in the process. Don't be the haphazard you. Be the smarter you. Set up a notebook *before* you begin.

Think back over the type of aquaponic garden you're most interested in building. Do you want a simple nutrient film with either the drip or ebb and flow type of watering? Do you want a deep water culture? Is the media-based grow bed more your style? Narrowing down your system takes this from theory to practice. You are one step closer to actually following through and creating your very own aquaponic garden.

Now, take it from theory into practicality. Sketch out or refine the garden of your dreams. Are you the scrounger? The engineer? The unicorn? The beginner with a hectic lifestyle needing the convenience of a kit? There is no one way to venture through the garden gate into aquaponic gardening. No one style is superior to another. There is only you, your lifestyle, the challenges that make your heart race with pleasure. Design a garden that is you or a combo of you and your partner.

Even if the time is not now, creating a sketch is your promise to yourself, *someday. Someday I will do this.* A sketch is the basis of your shopping list. By putting it down on paper and realizing what you need to find or purchase, you have fashioned a checklist. You can watch for sales and put together a box with all your bits and pieces much more economically if you do this over time. Nothing spells defeat faster than a bottom line beyond your means. And that needn't be the case.

Decide on your fish and on your plants. This is where it all becomes a sparkle in your eye. This carries you from the fear of starting to the gigantic first step of construction. That first step is the only step that matters. I believe in the adage, *well begun is half done*. If you don't start you can't finish. It's just that simple. You have to take the first step in cutting pipes or washing gravel, some deliberate action that takes the theoretical into the physical.

Take some time creating the perfect water before you plant. You know by now that the nutrient-laden water holds the magic of growth. Don't rush through this all important step in the process. Success is what primes the system for continued growth, expanding your enterprise, dreaming of bigger and better systems. Rushing is the death knell to all of your invested time and money.

Begin experimenting with recipes. It will whet your appetite for more healthy food and encourage you to start your experiment. Collect other recipes you love and let it form the basis for a healthier you, a healthier family. The lifestyle you develop may very well save you from the ravaging effects of diabetes or heart disease. Each healthy step you take is cemented into a healthier body and an invitation to continue on the journey to a stronger version of *you*.

Spend some time reviewing the glossary. This is the overflow of extra wisdom you can cull as you go from your first taste of aquaponics to the advanced status of master gardener. You may have skimmed over much of the glossary at the beginning, wanting to digest each chapter as you flipped through the pages. That's okay. Just don't settle for a little knowledge. Understanding the underlying concepts is just as important as the initial reading.

And finish by going through the pictures again. One of those pictures resonated with you. It was a system you wanted the most. Look at it, and use it as your wish list for a garden of your own, a year round garden that never dies with winter's hoary breath. Pictures stimulate our hearts and minds, and I've given you many to salivate over.

I'm proud of you for sticking with it and reading the whole book. You have learned so much. Your family and friends will be thrilled with the outcome, and most importantly, so will you. Achievement is the highest form of growing self-reliance and self-confidence. Your knowledge and experience make you the expert everyone will turn to when they want to replicate your aquaponic garden. You're a rock star! Join some online groups and share what you know. The new friends you'll make will be people just like you. They're waiting for you!

www.ingramcontent.com/pod-product-compliance
Lightning Source LLC
Chambersburg PA
CBHW050318120526
44592CB00014B/1962